Published by Lulu Publishing & Limelight Publishing.
Copyright © 2020 Demene Benjamin
Cover design by Hammad at Fiverr
All Rights Reserved.

ISBN 978-1-71655-406-3
lulu.com
limelightpublishing.com

Demene Benjamin split her young life between the suburbs of Pittsburgh, Pennsylvania and the City of Tampa. As a child she enjoyed writing poetry and discovering her uniqueness amongst a family of 6. She has always been passionate and loves to encourage, motivate and support those around her.

Recently finishing her Education Specialist Degree, Demene is the author of several published poems, the Journal of My Reflection series and the UrEsteem blog and non-profit organization which are geared toward building mental health, love and self-esteem.

She is an avid community partner who desires to impact youth and bring out positive change through various outlets including projects, events and workshops.

I hope you enjoy the newest journal from UrEsteem. May you find your true colors as you color, write and draw through this book. It is our purpose to help you discover that you are a truly unique and beautiful individual; a true masterpiece!

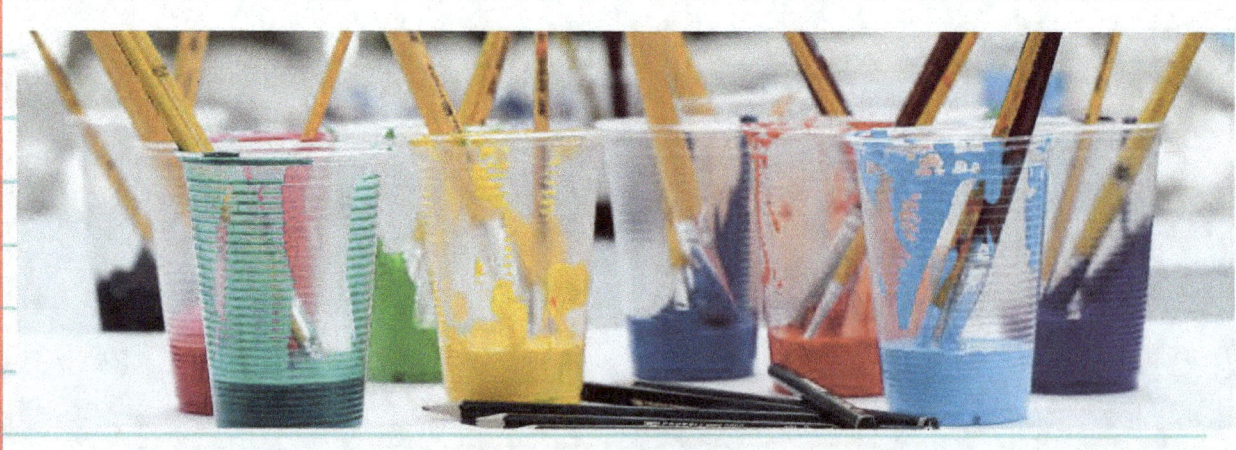

Take time to color

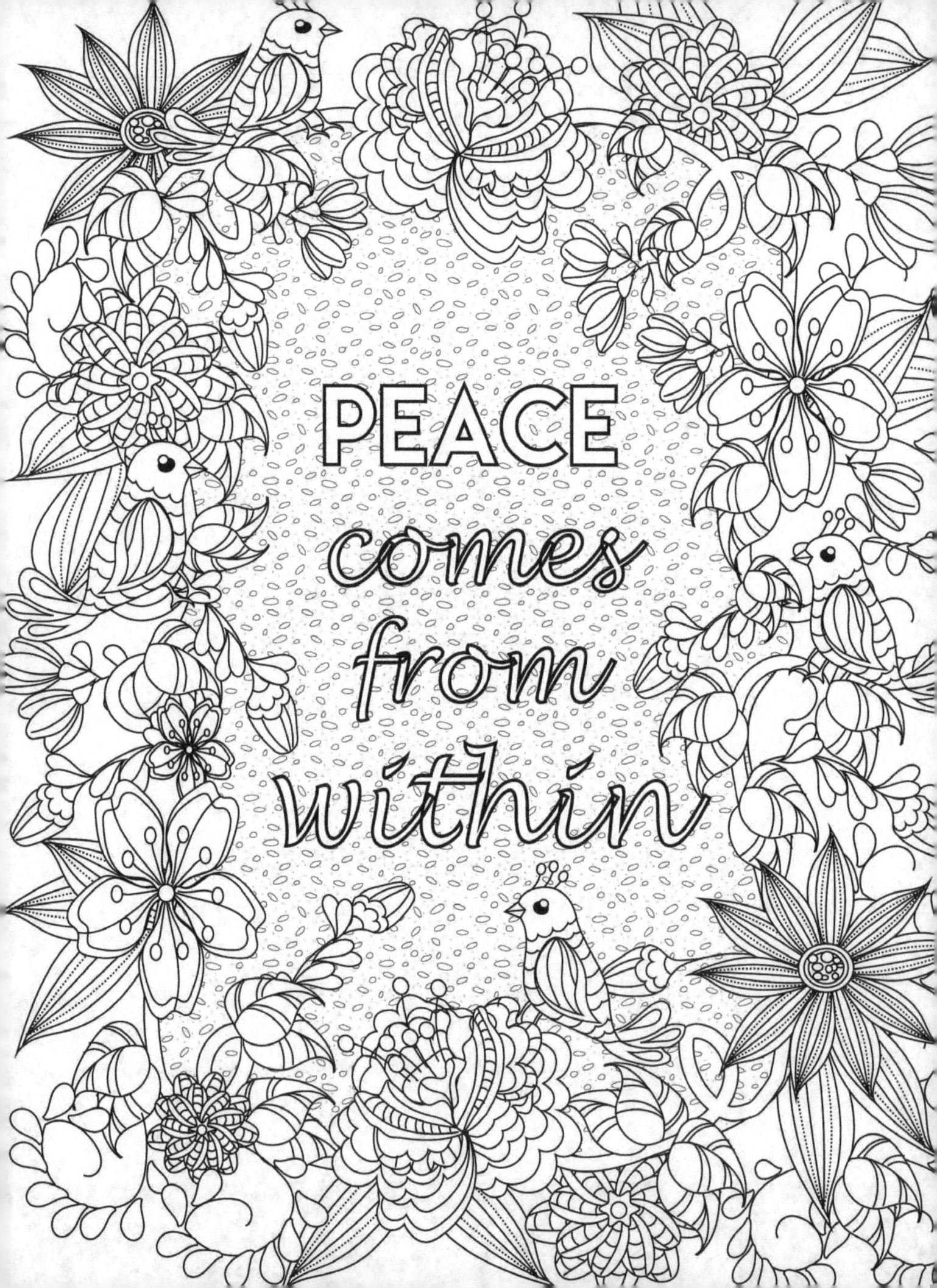

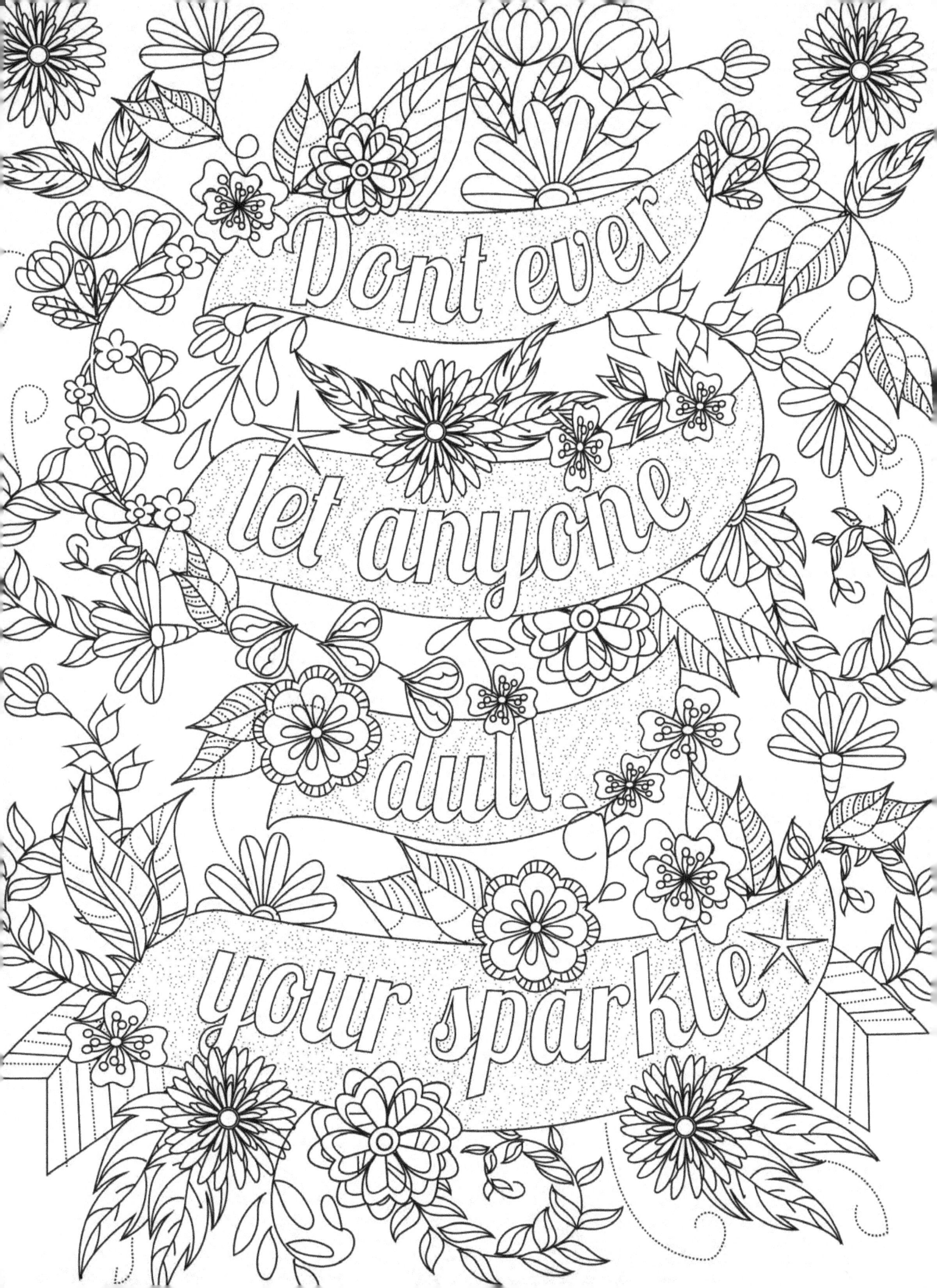

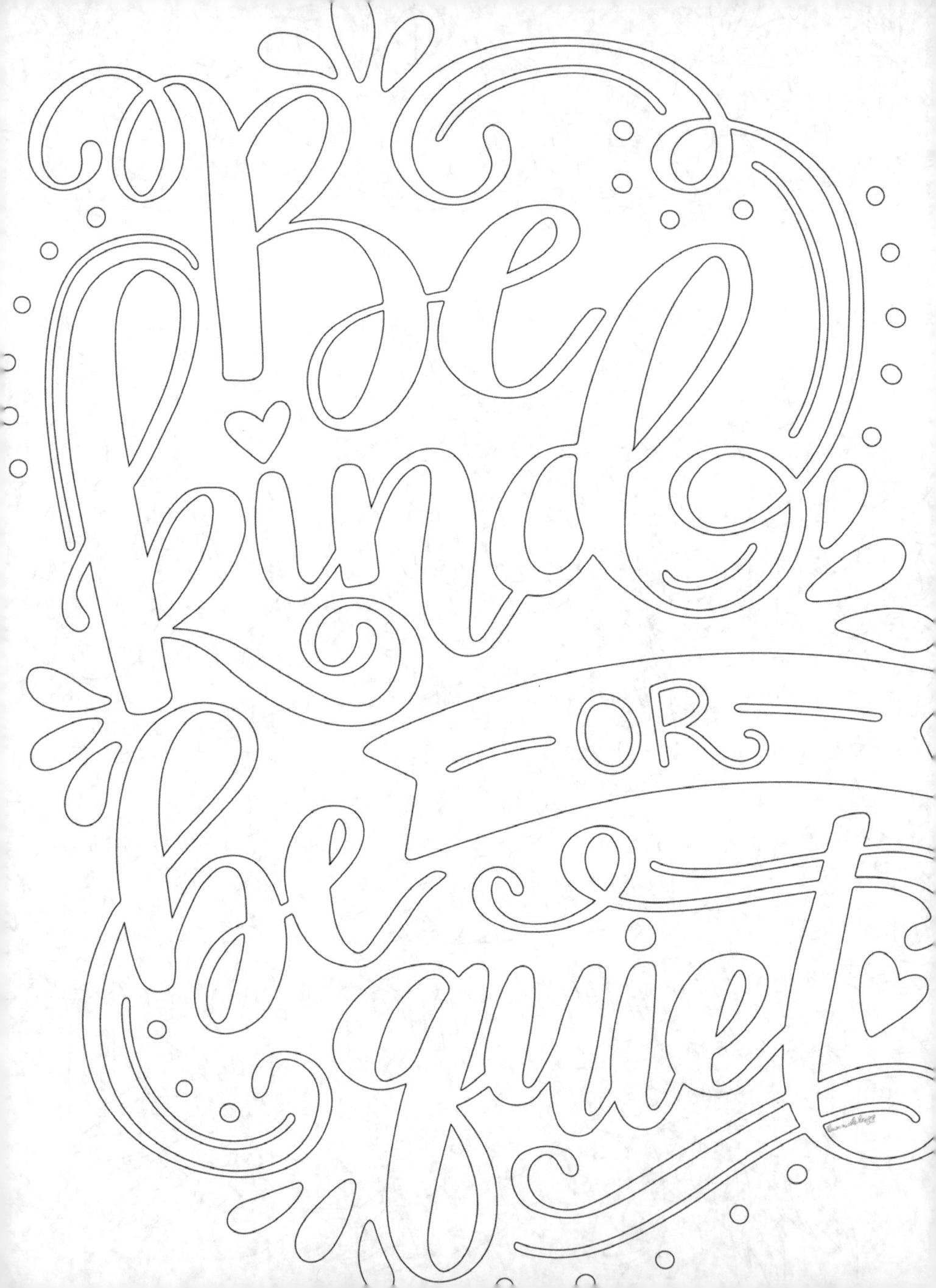

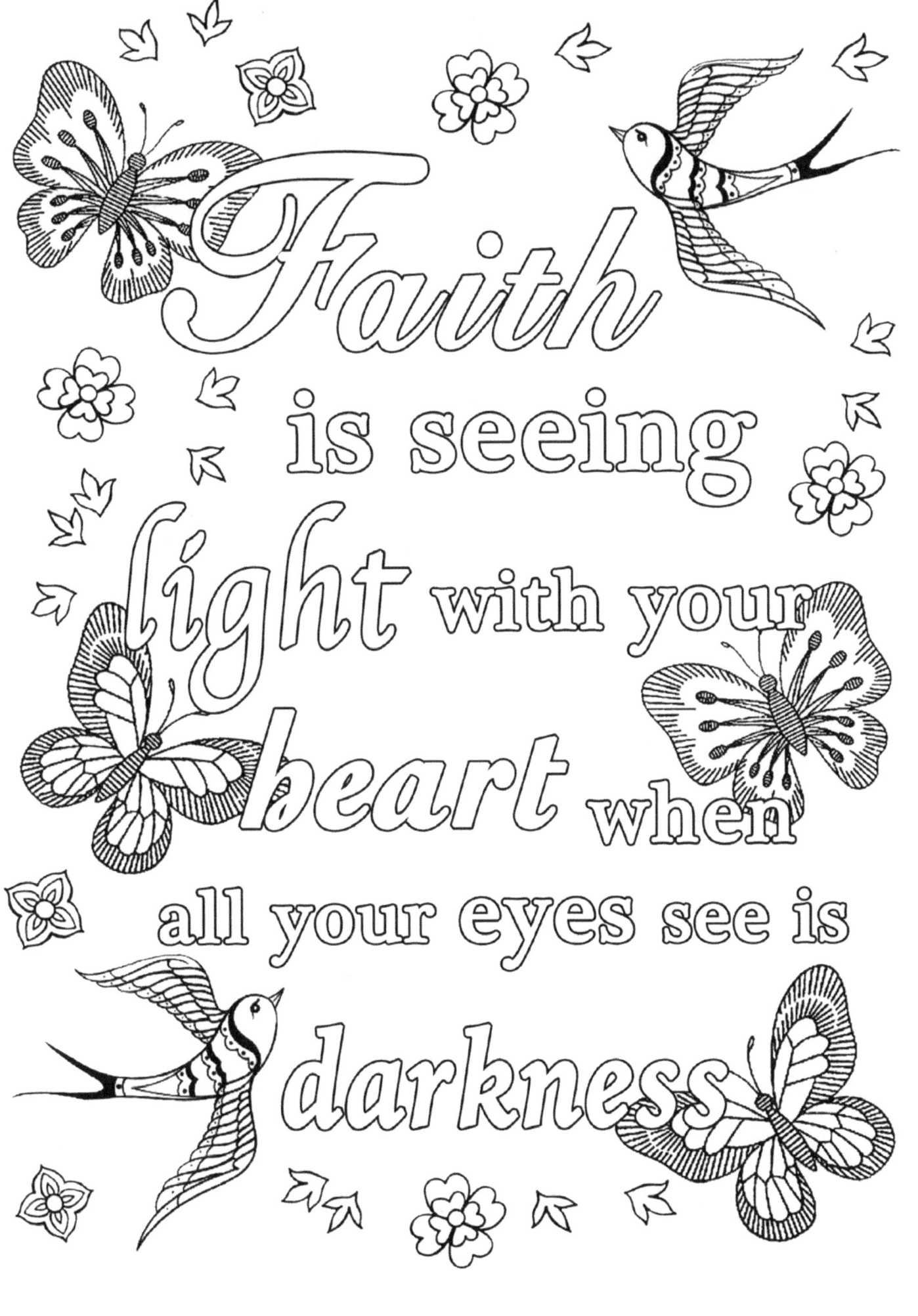

Faith is seeing light with your heart when all your eyes see is darkness

Draw a big heart and divide it into 6 sections. Fill each section with the things or people that fill your heart (what/who you love).

Fill the page with some of your favorite emoji's. Why are these your favorite emotions.

Exercise is good for the mind and body.
Draw a picture to represent your mind, and
body. Write about your favorite exercise
and how it makes you feel.

Have you ever had to wait in line or keep trying something? Practice playing with a puzzle or doing origami. Draw a ruler across the paper and think of a few things that you have to stop, think, practice and repeat. Write them down.

Write down 10 things about yourself. Draw pictures for 4 of the things.

TAKE TIME TO COLOR

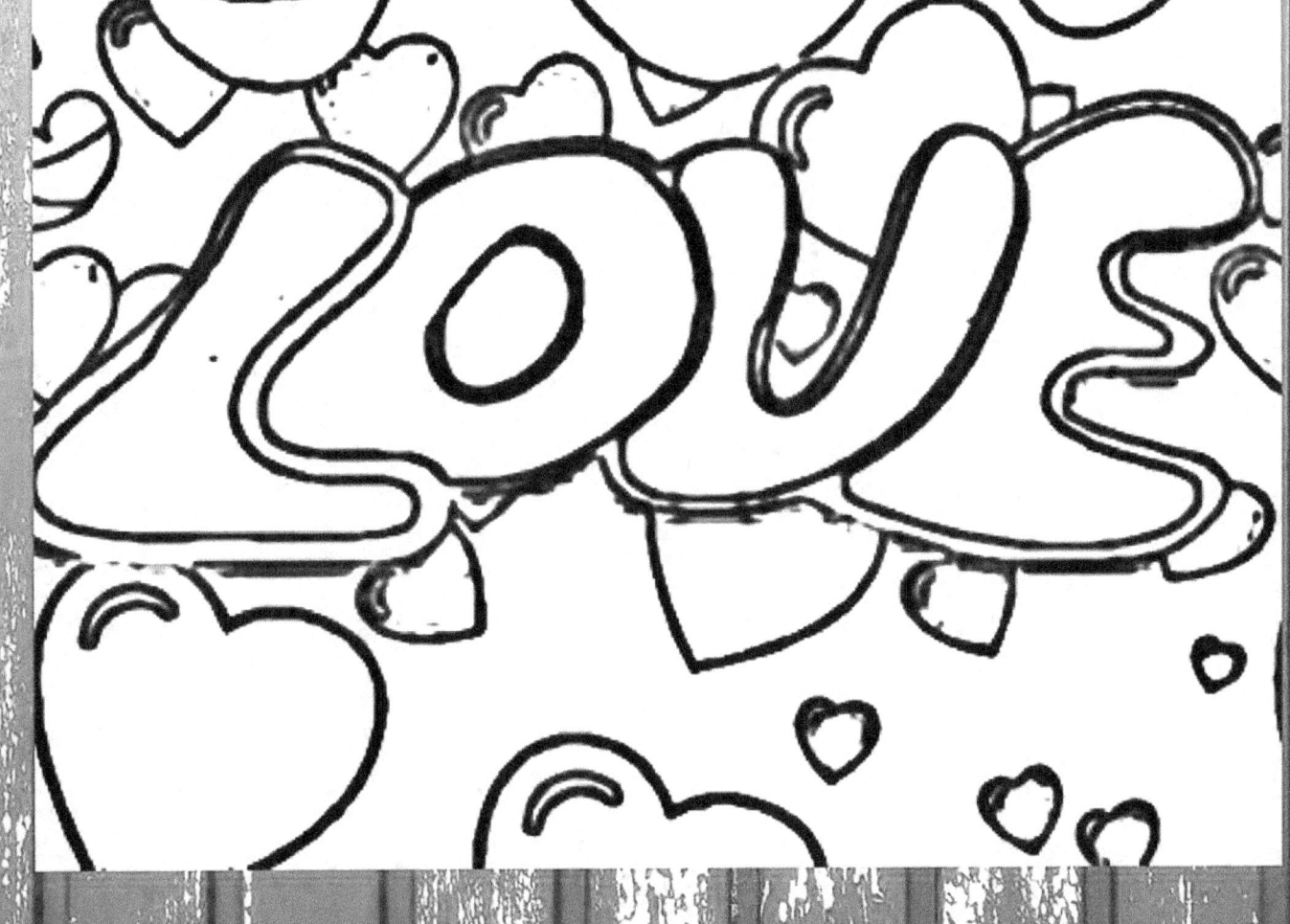

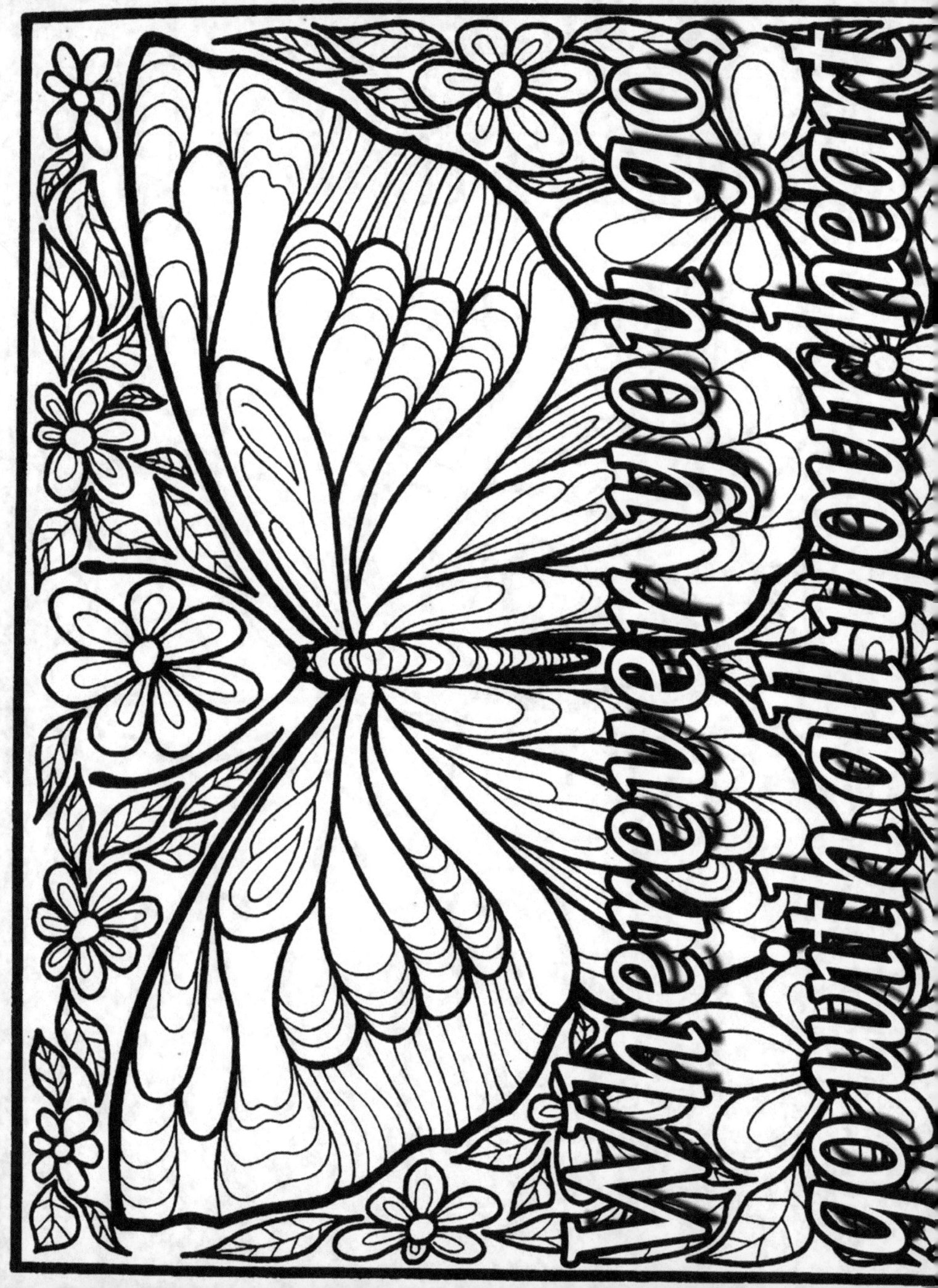

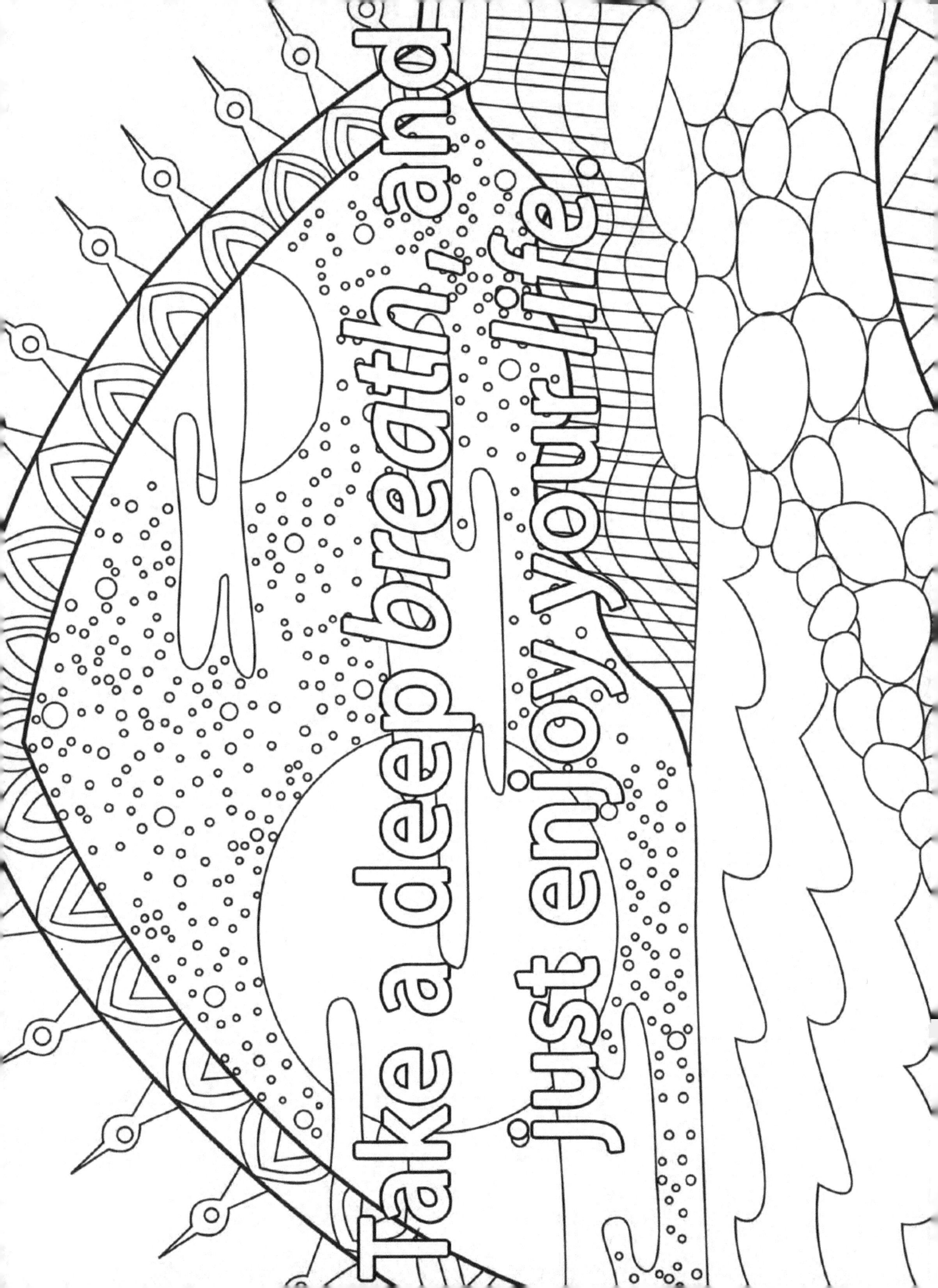

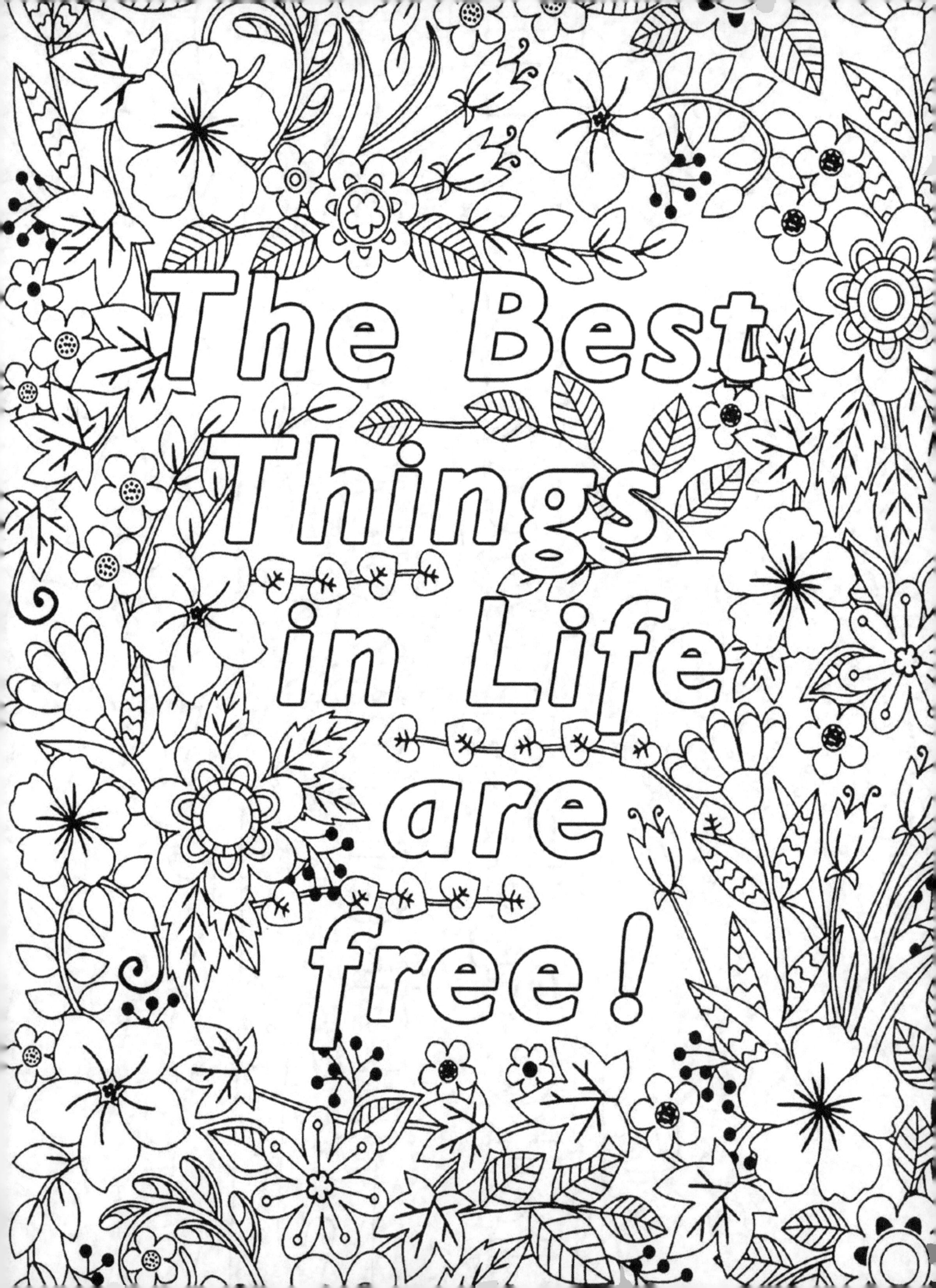

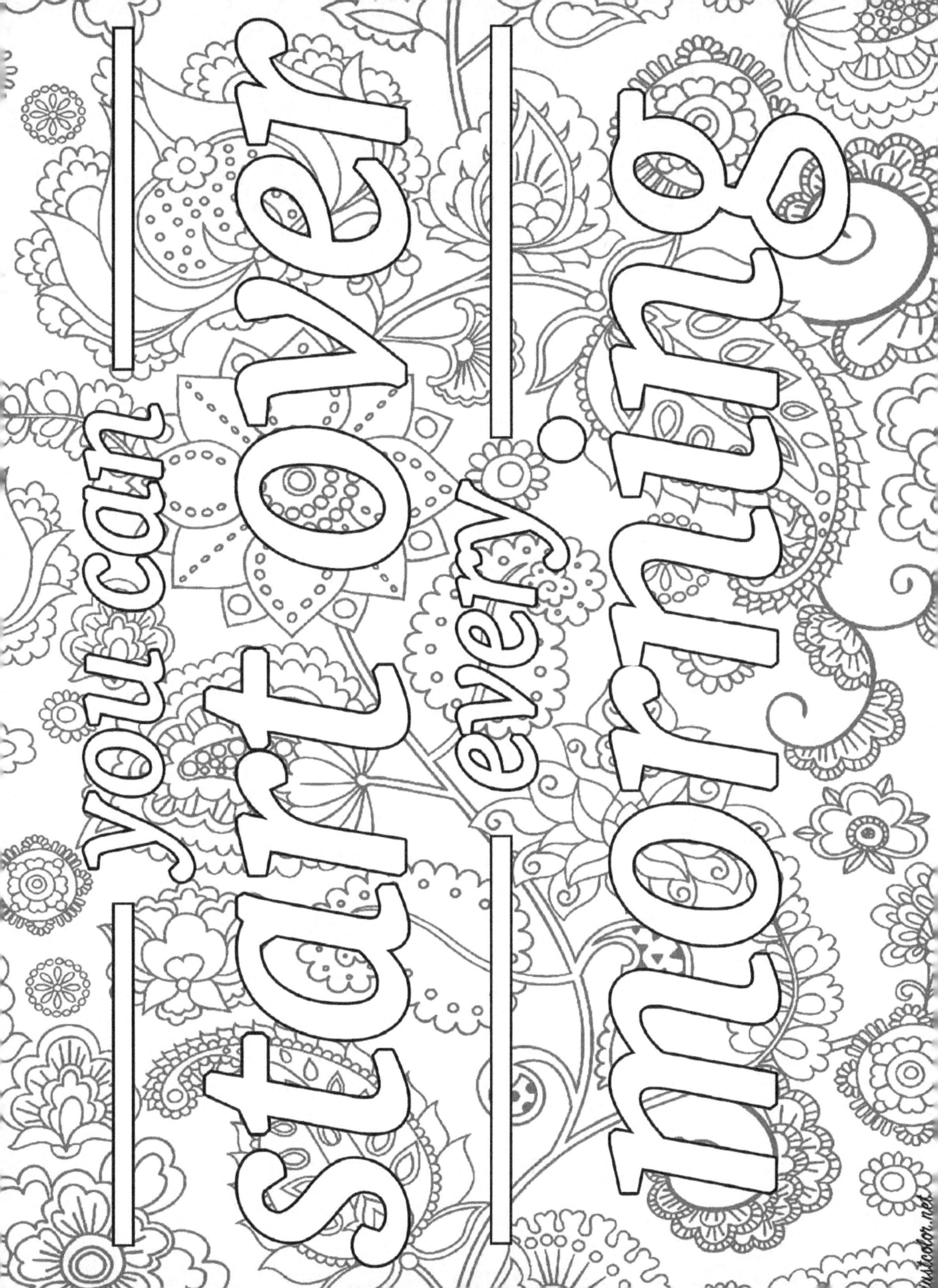

Time to go fishing for compliments. Write 10 nice things about your family. Draw and color a few fish on your page.

If you were a music note, what note would you be? Draw the note in the middle of the page. Think of a few songs that you like and write your favorite around the note.

How does the music make you feel?

Write about what makes you ANGRY. Get the red color pencil out and express yourself. Be sure to include how you express your anger..

Do you like your behavior when your angry?

What is your favorite movie? What do you like about it? What was your favorite part?

Make a list of 20 things you want to do.
Shade each entry with a different color.

Take time to color

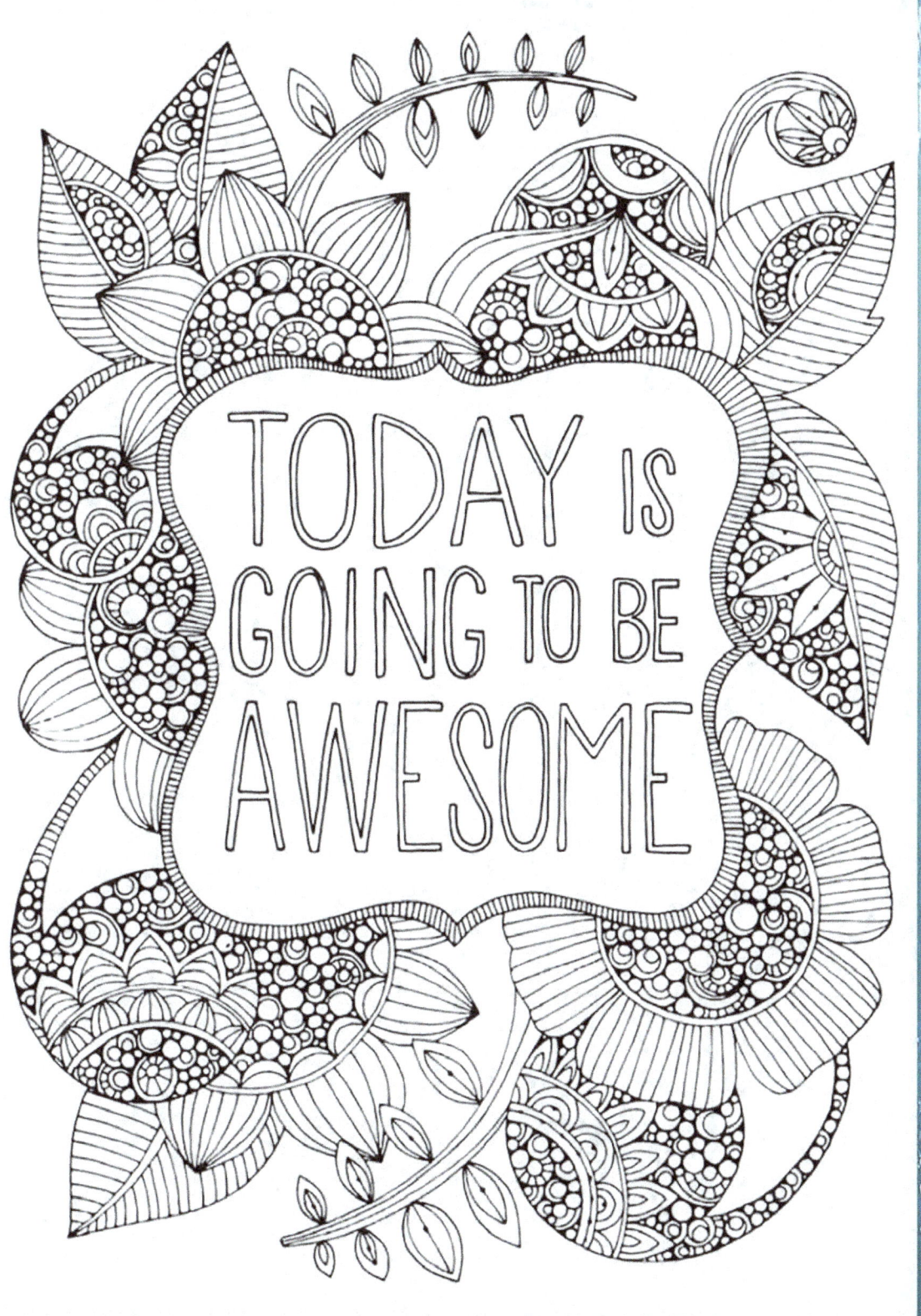

TODAY IS GOING TO BE AWESOME

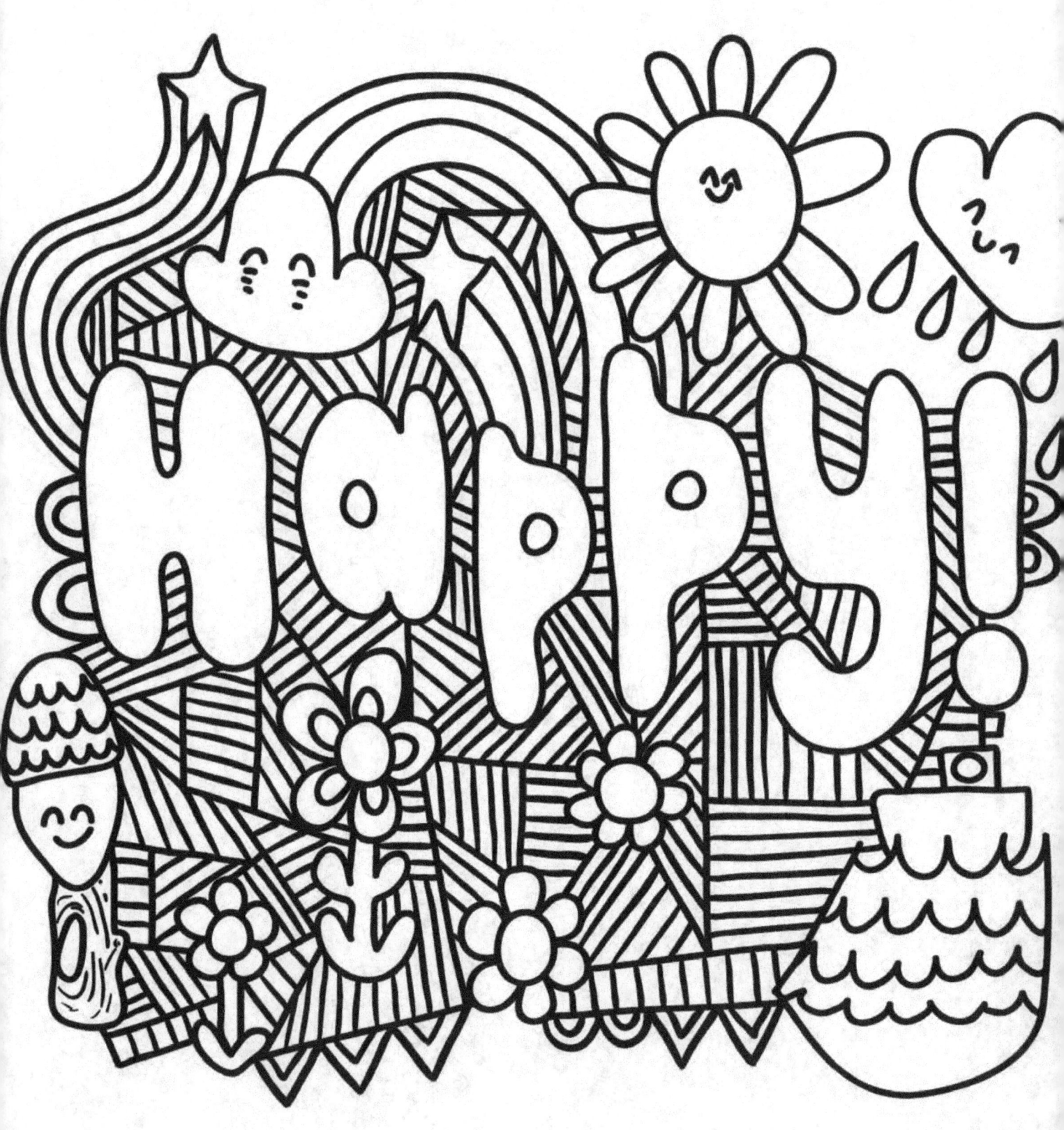

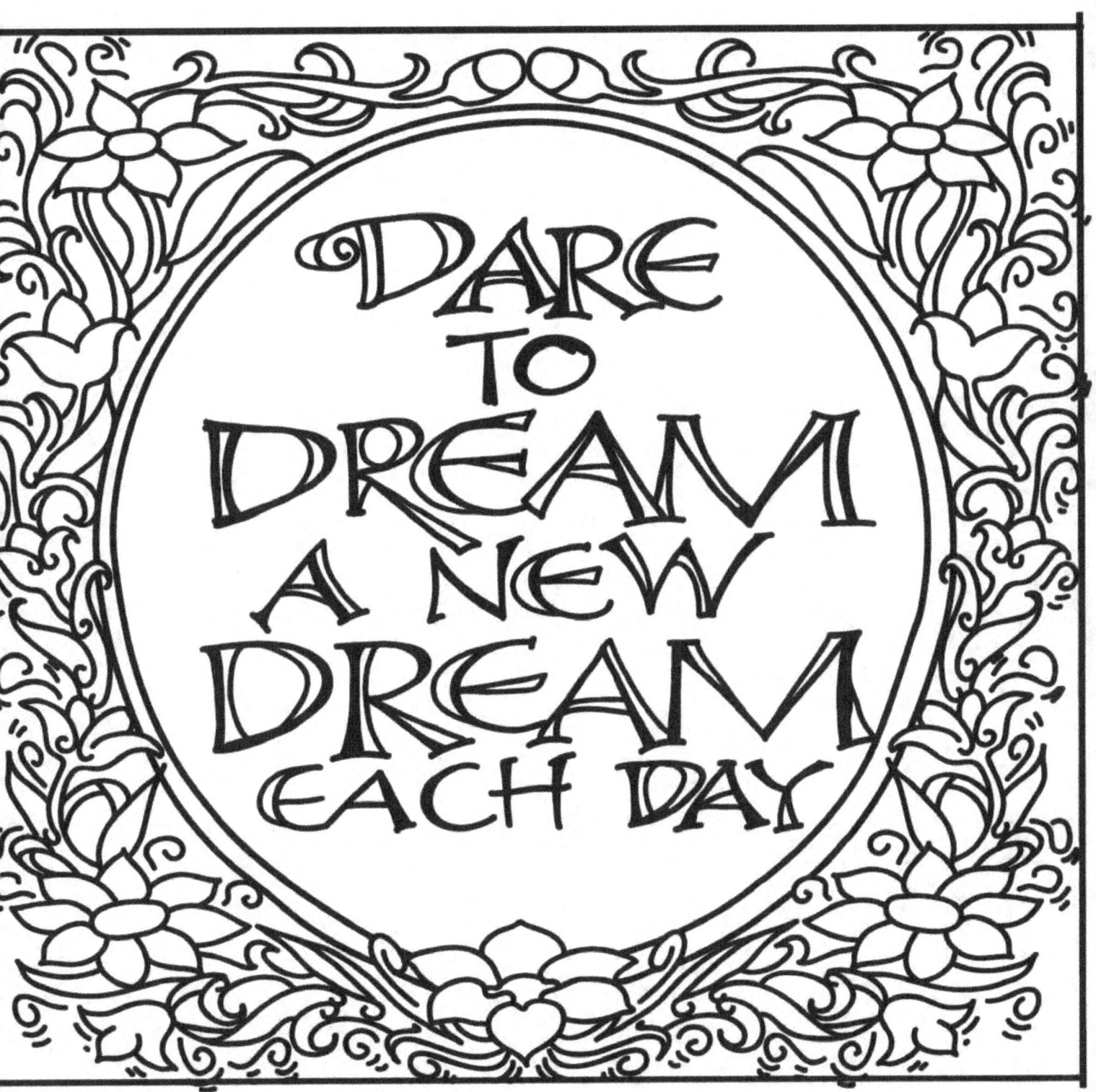

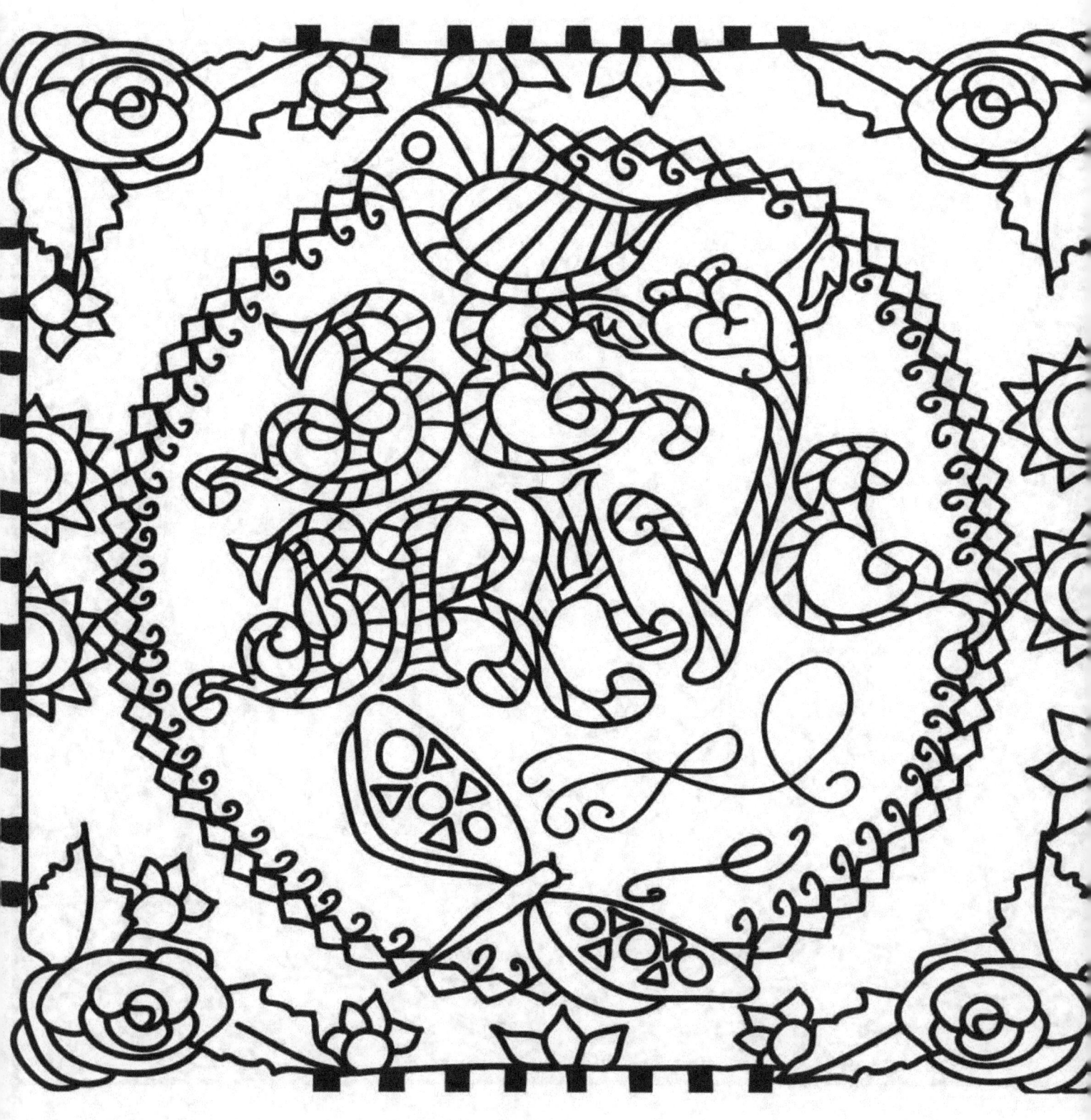

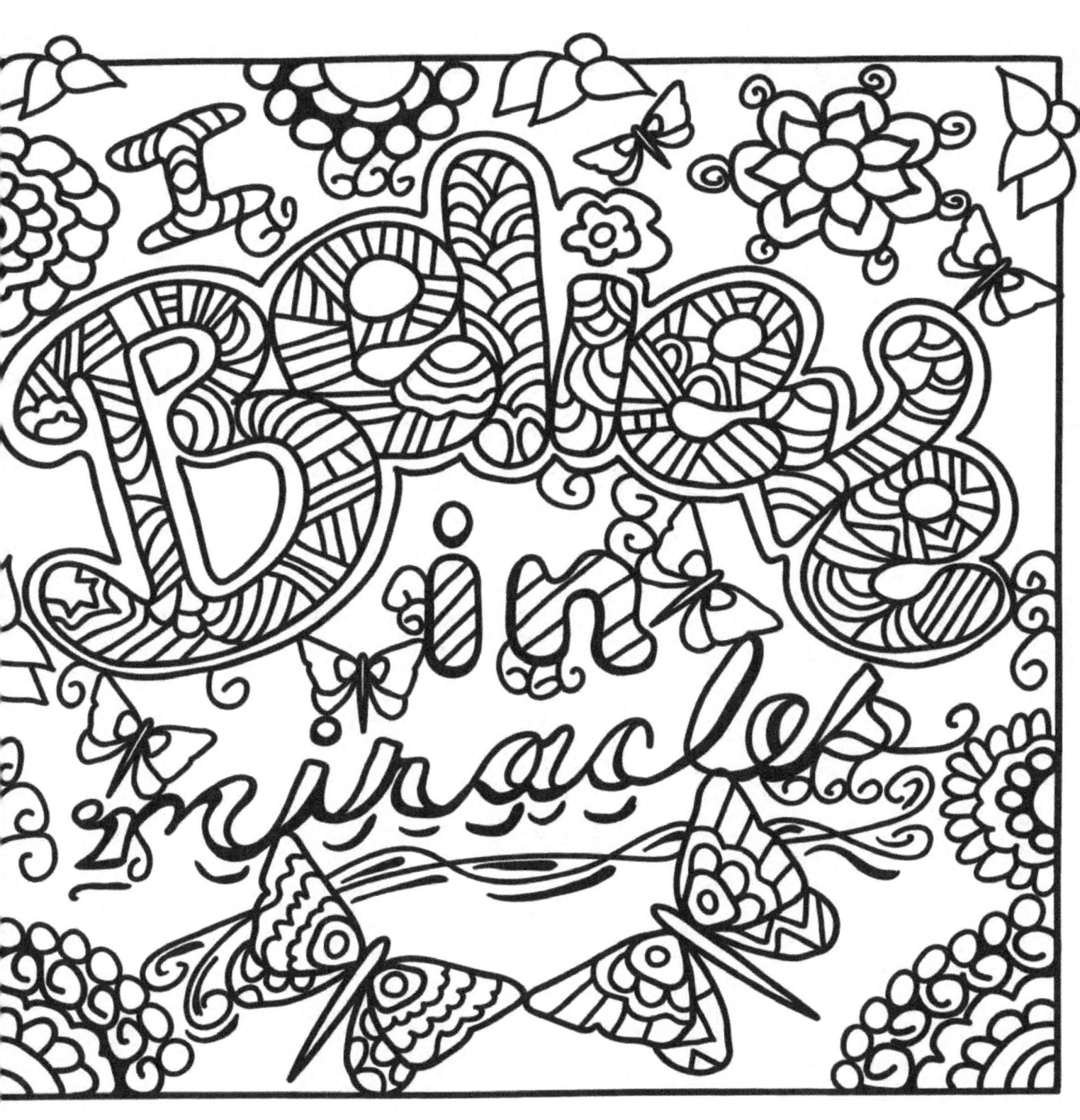

Write a letter to yourself. In the letter describe what you look like. At the bottom of your page add a selfie.

Write down what you ate yesterday. Circle the items in red that are not healthy and the healthy items in green. Draw a few healthy items on your page.

Draw a garden. Find a flower and press it in your book.

Staying positive takes work. Draw a big gas tank on your page and fill it with 10 positive words or pictures.

What is your favorite color? Why? Fill the page with your favorite color.

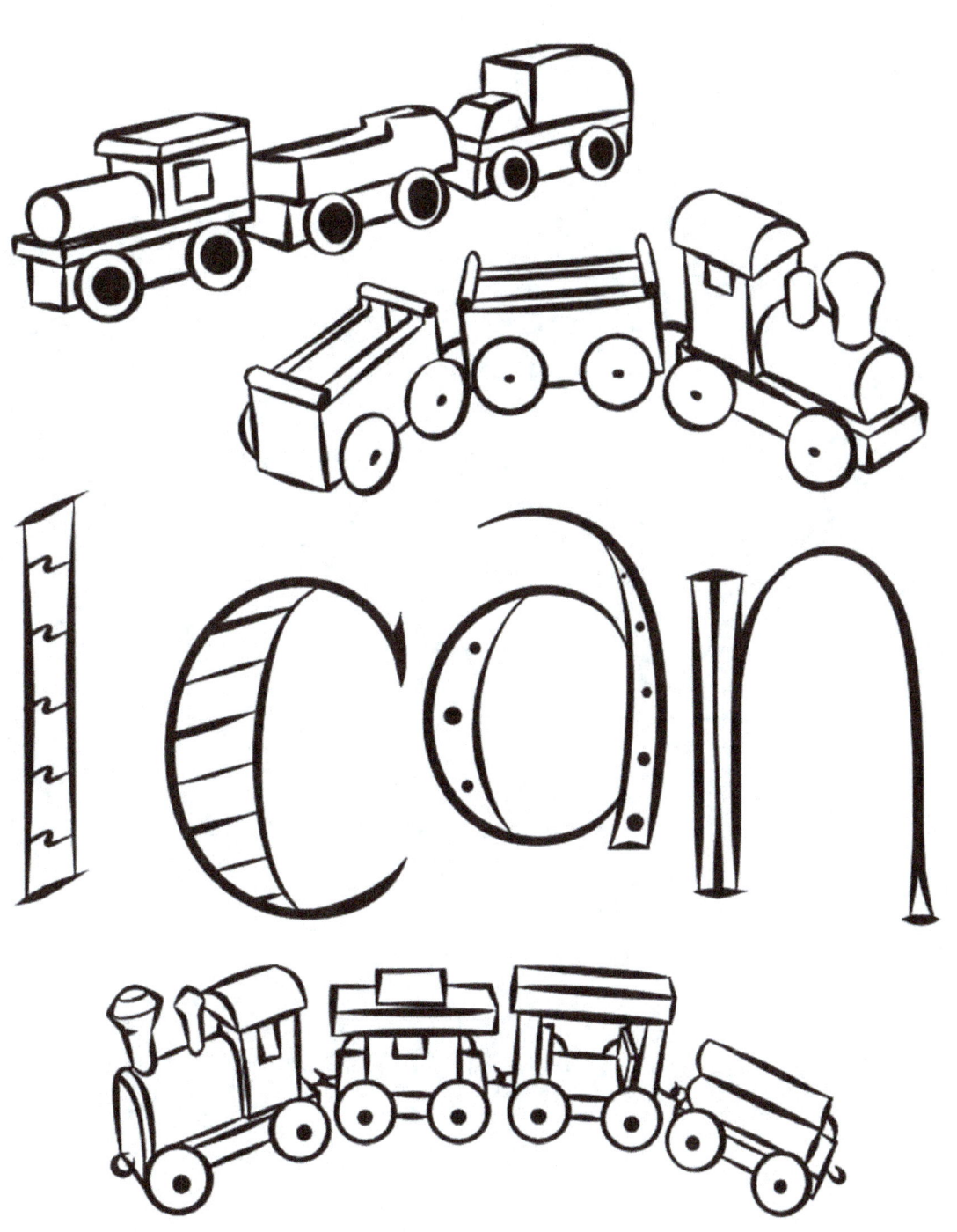

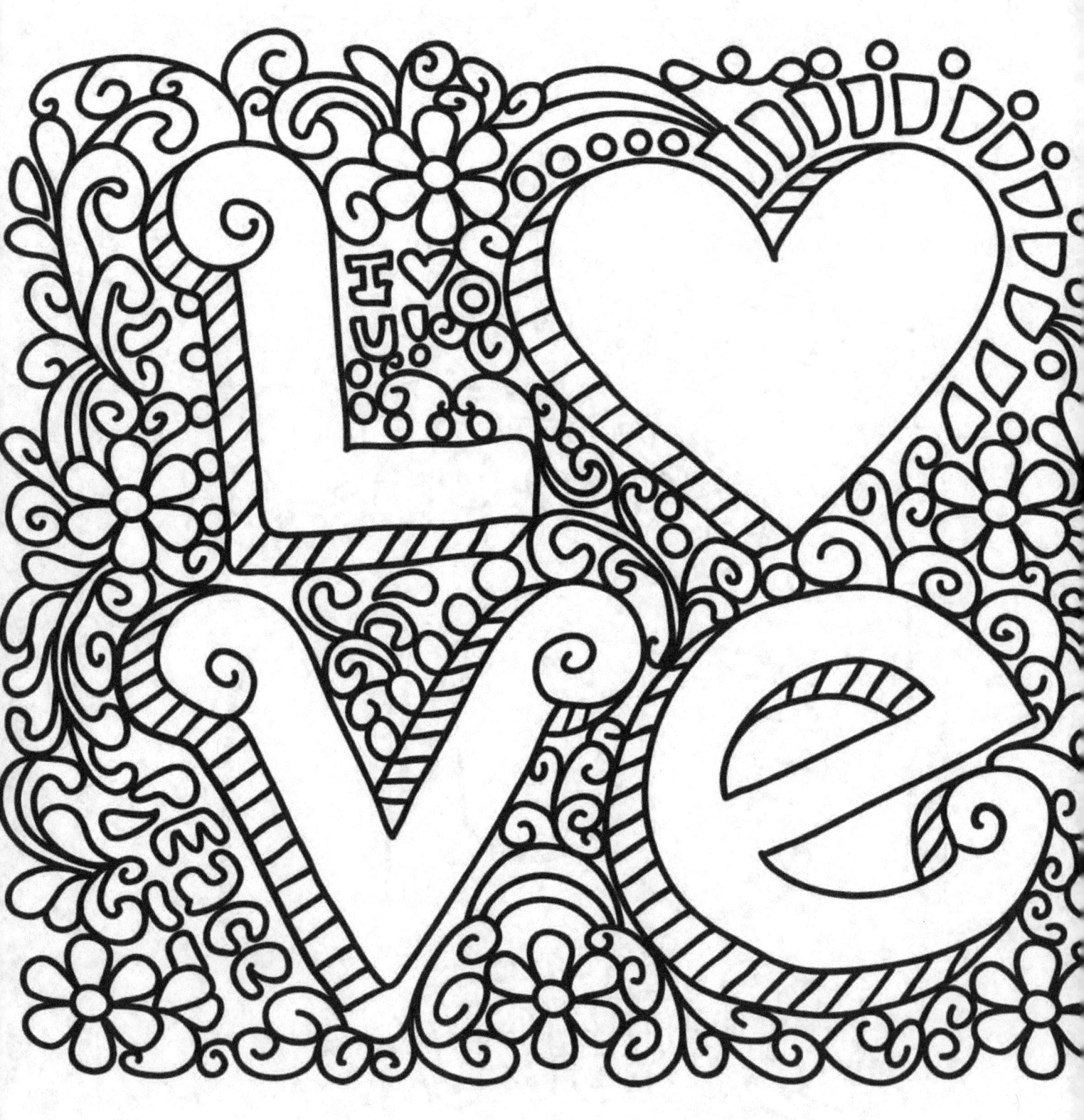

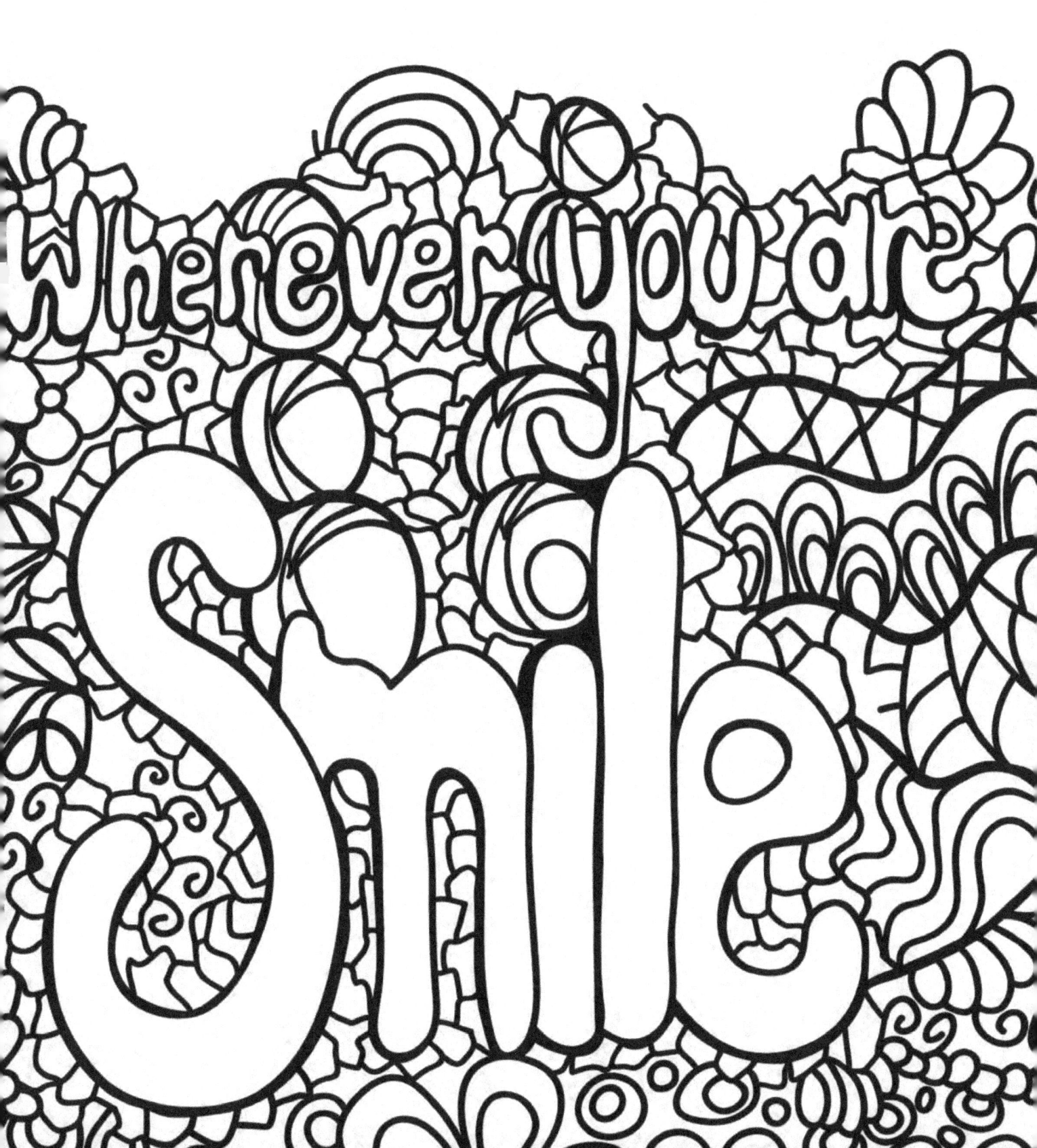

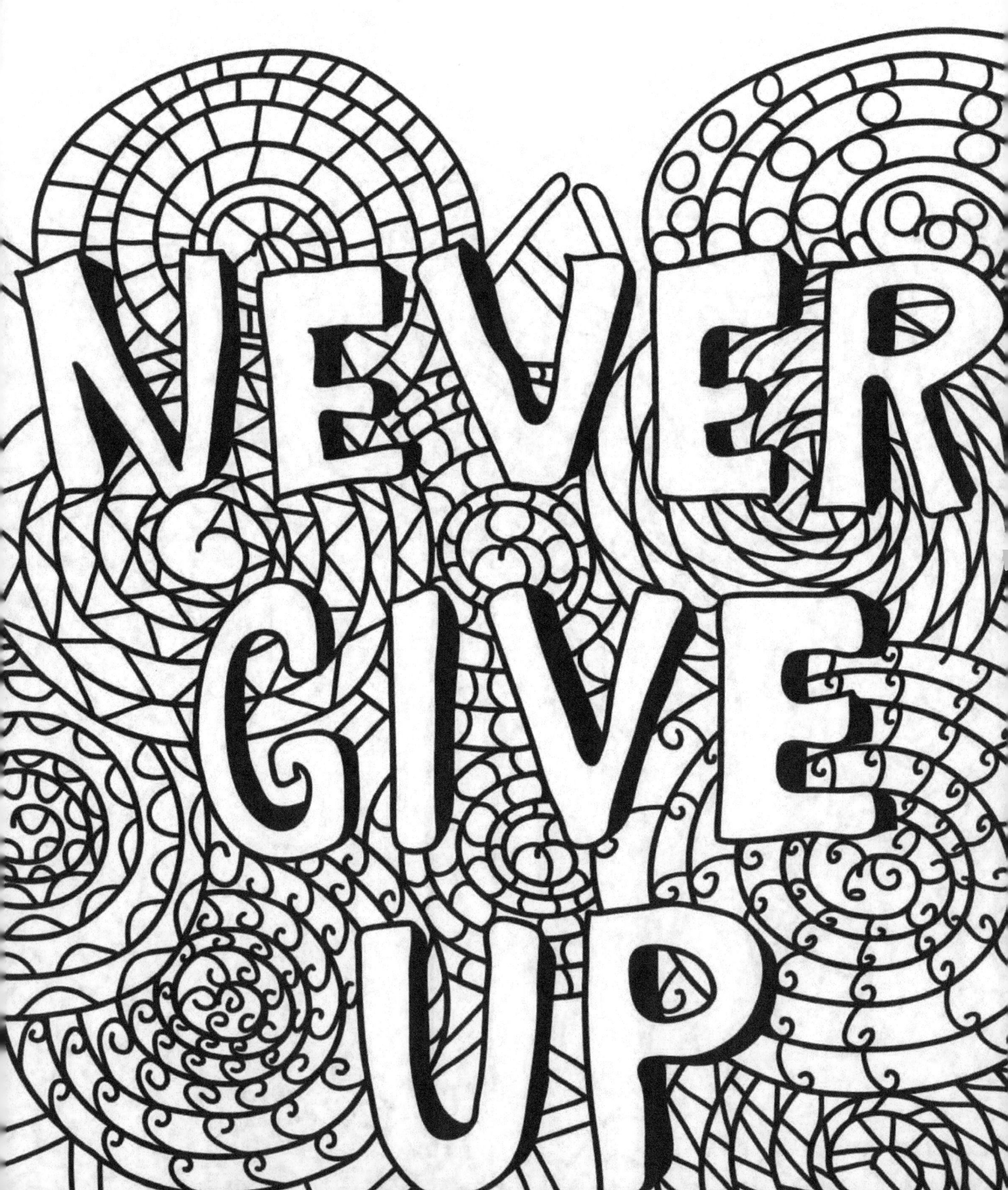

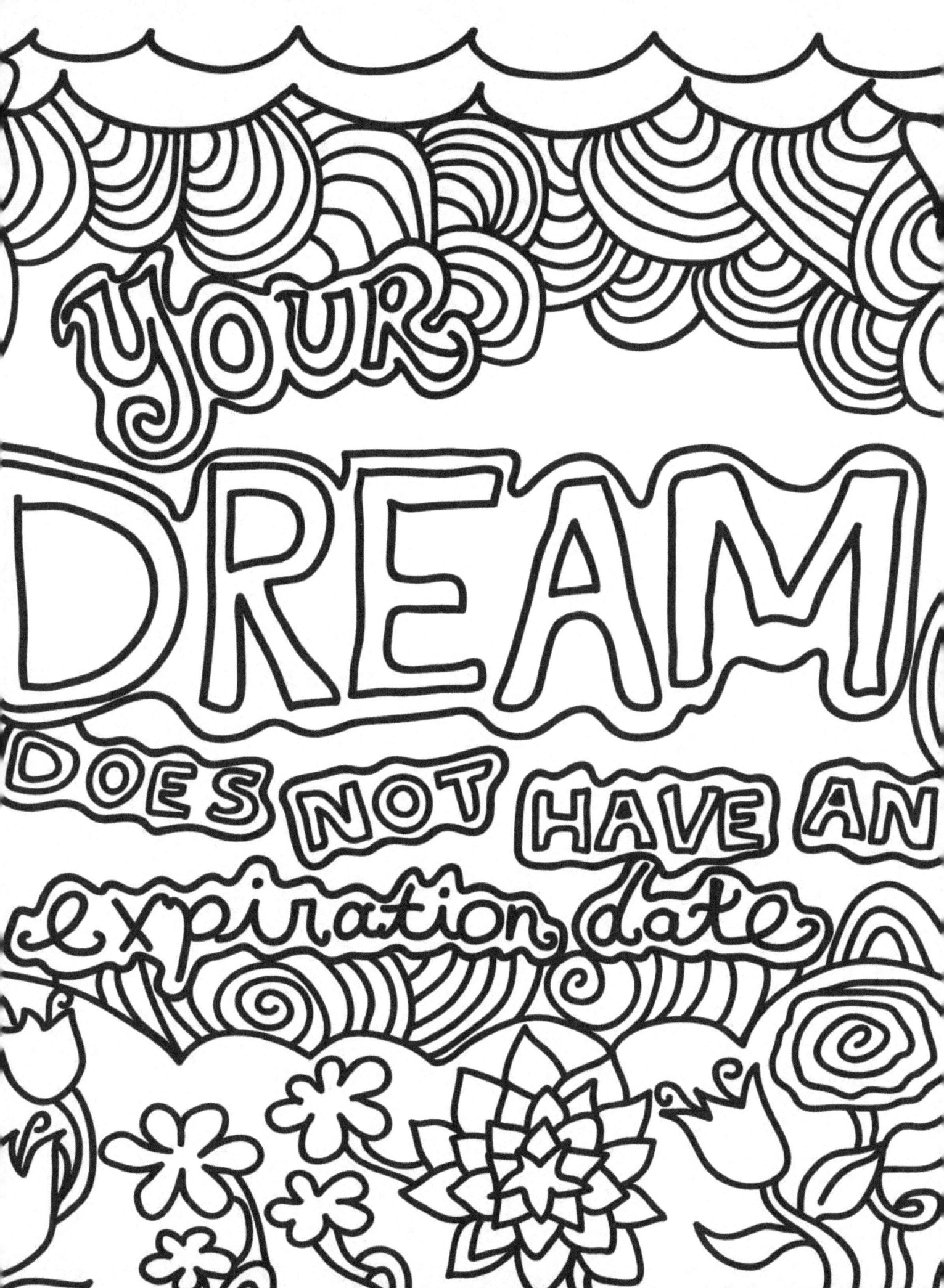

Take a moment to just relax and doodle.

Who do you spend time with? What are
some things you do to have fun together?

Draw 9 squares on your page. Design and color all 9 squares.

What are you grateful for?

Write a letter to yourself that starts with, "I am". Talk about what you are going to do today, 3 years from now and 10 years from now. How old will you be? Draw something special on your page about yourself.

Take time to color

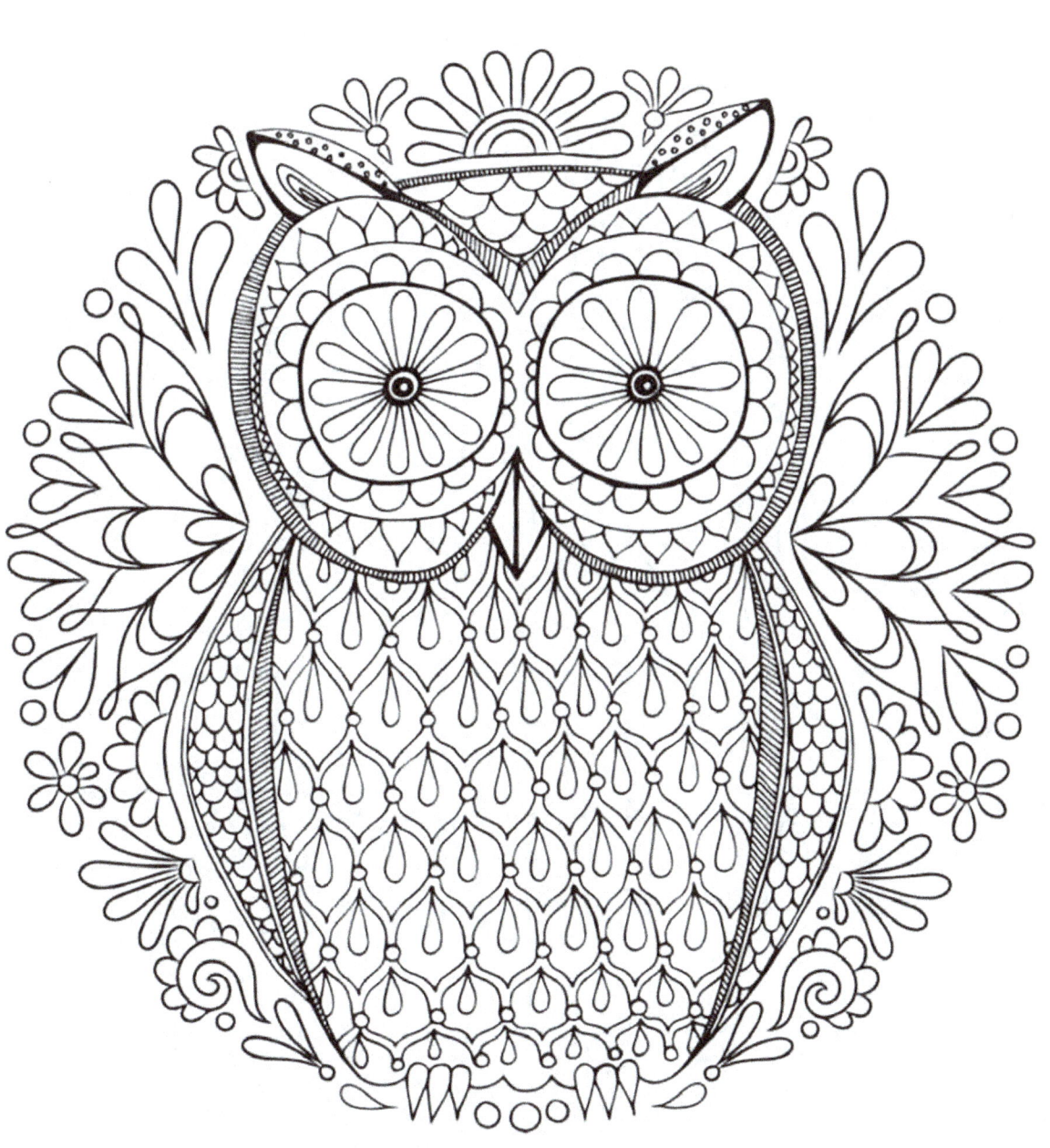

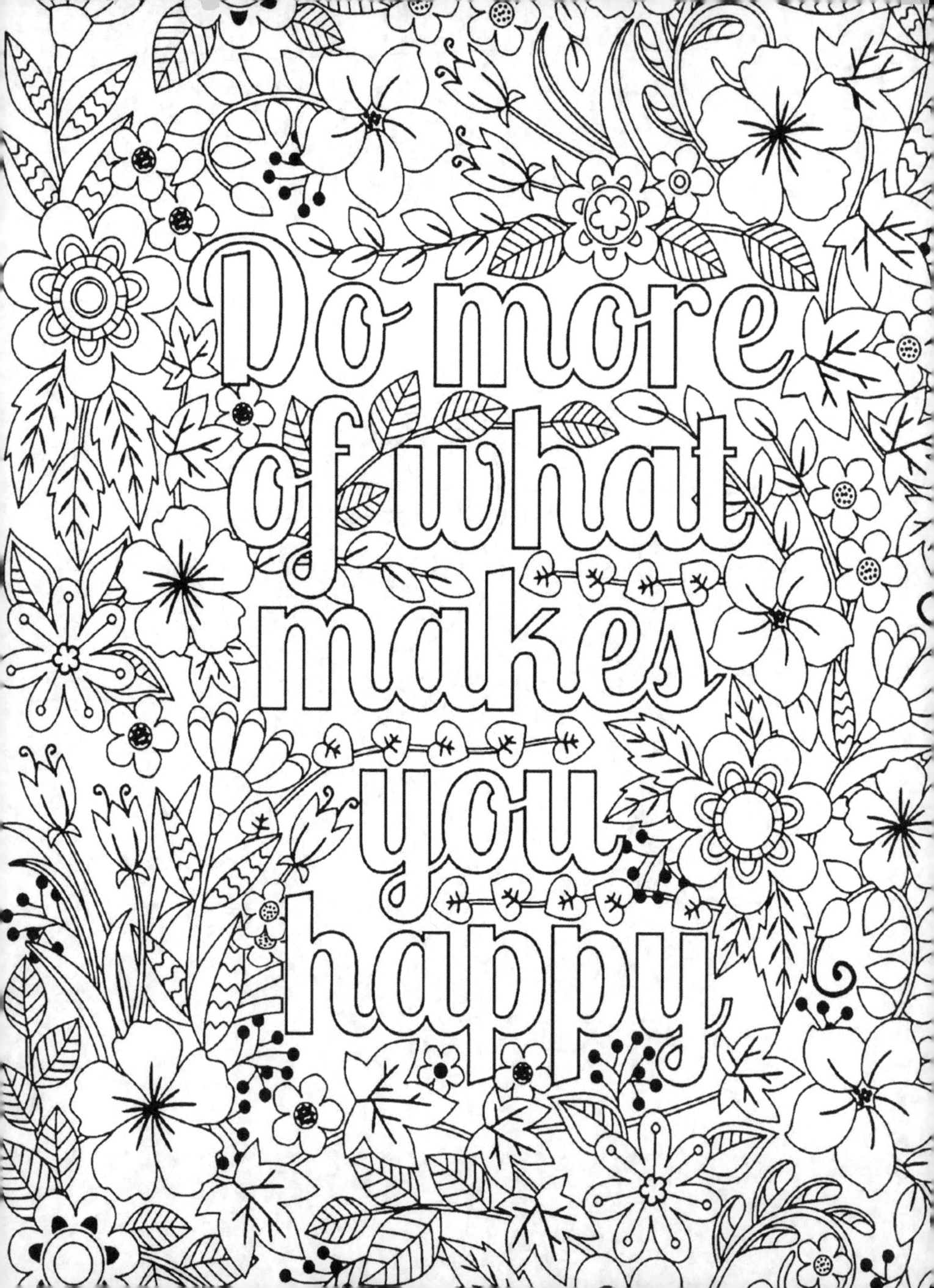

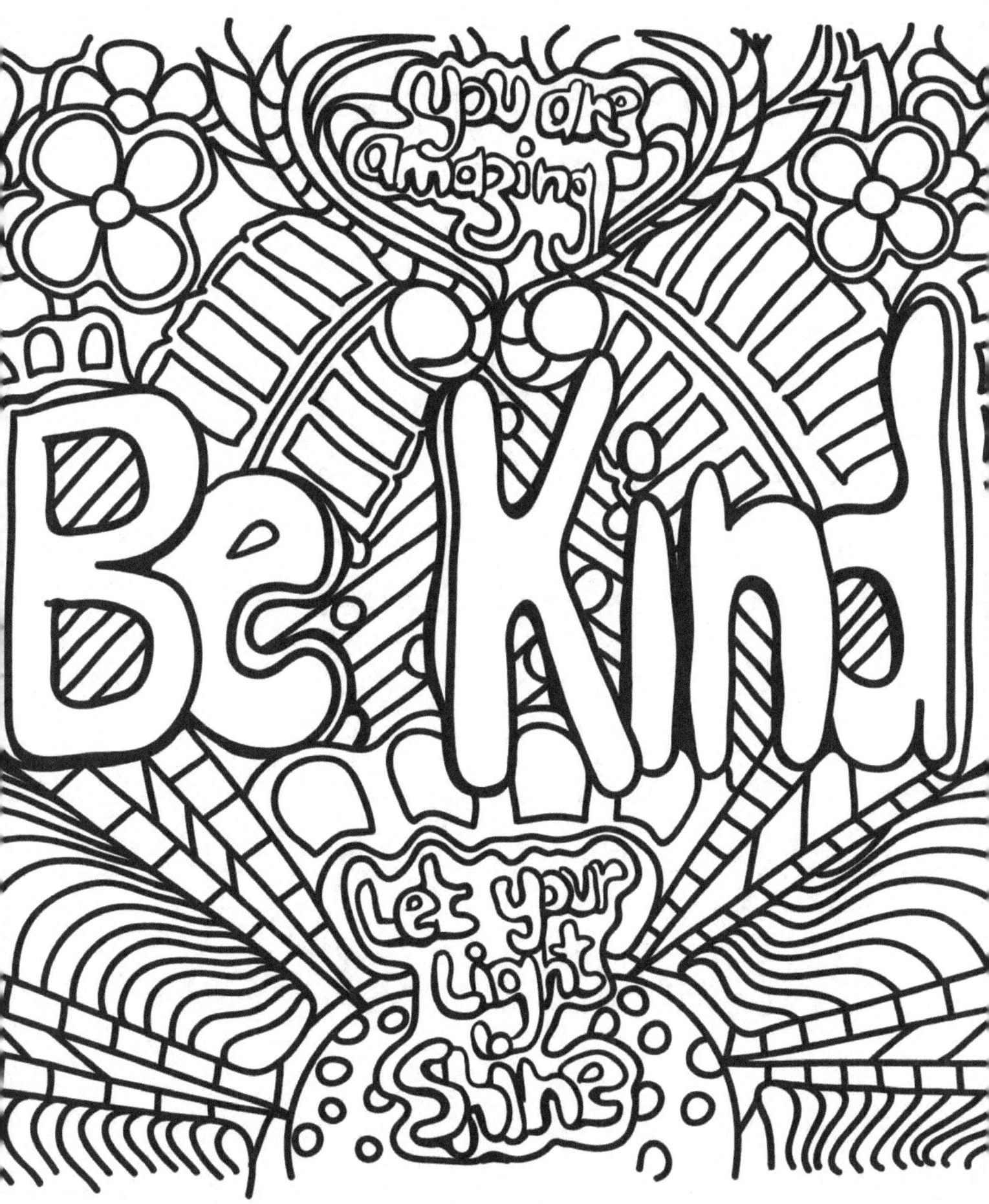

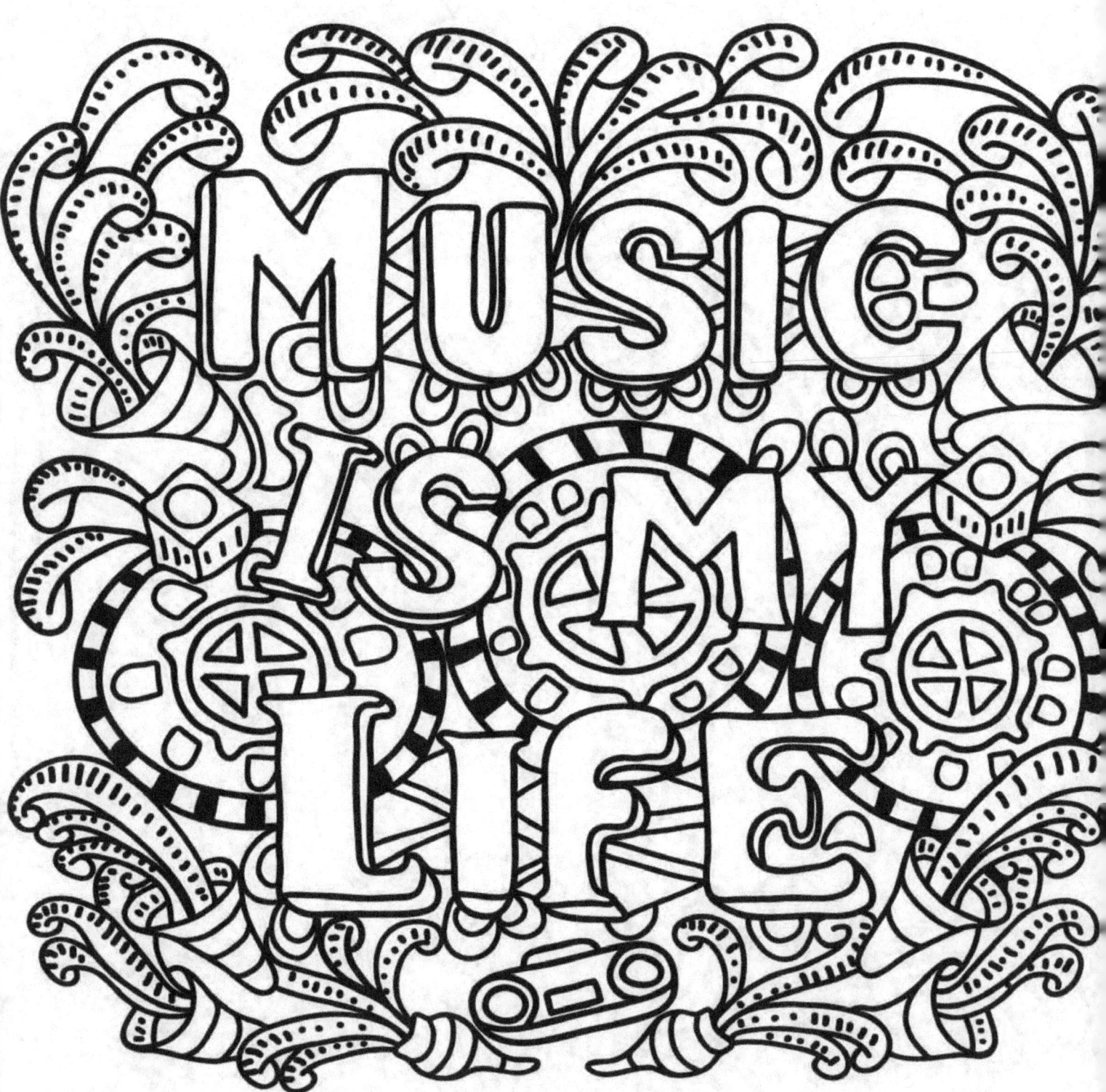

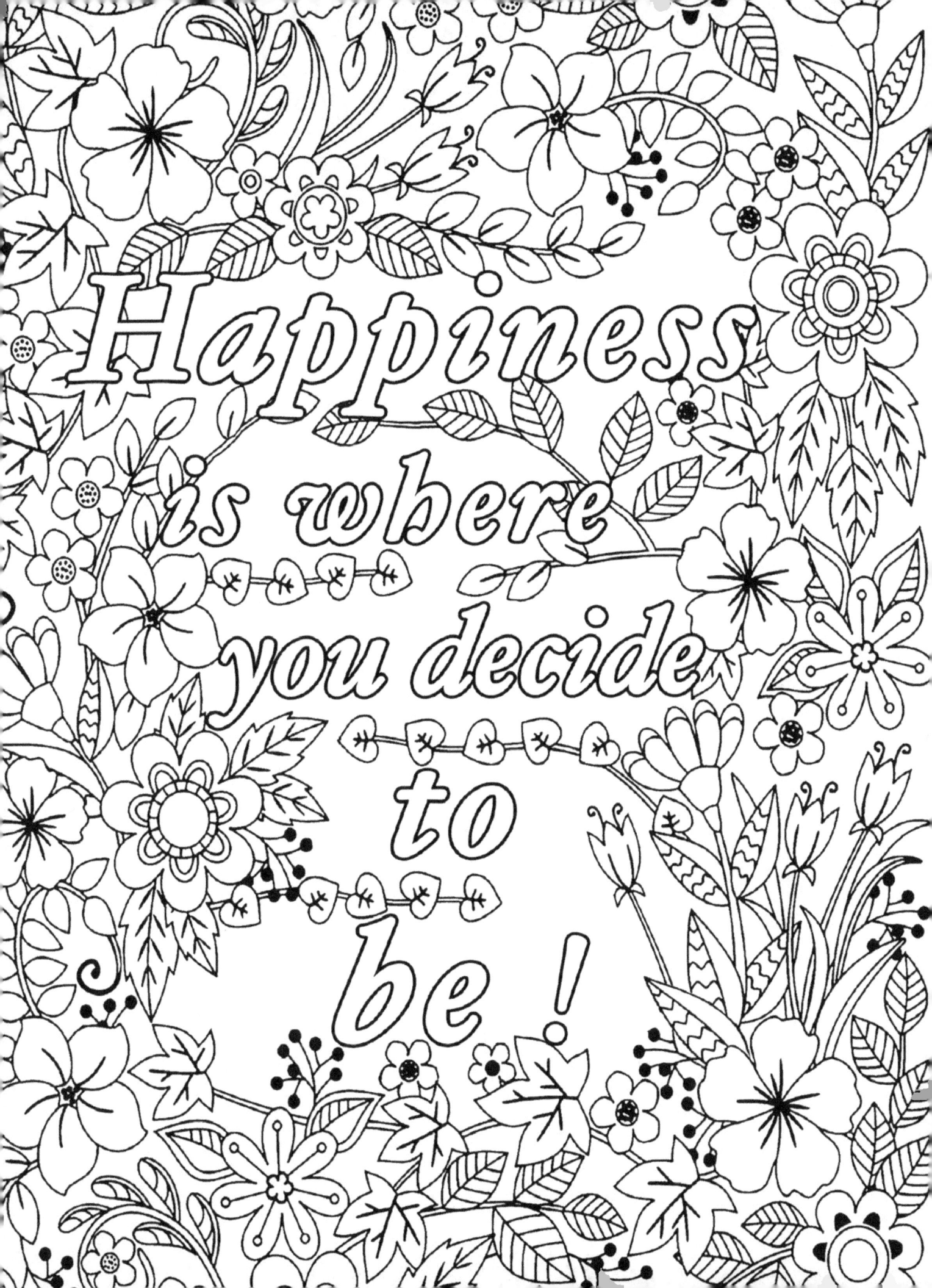

Free Write.

Take a moment to yourself and relax. Think about a few things you like to do when your alone and write them down.

Words are powerful! They can make you feel good or they can hurt you. Draw a sword and a heart on your page. Write down words under each picture that can express love or be hurtful. Shade the hurtful side in gray.

Are you ever afraid? Write down a few things that scare you. We have to learn to face our fears, so draw a big pair of eyes at the bottom of the page.

Think of a few things you do everyday. Do you enjoy doing these things?

Take time to color

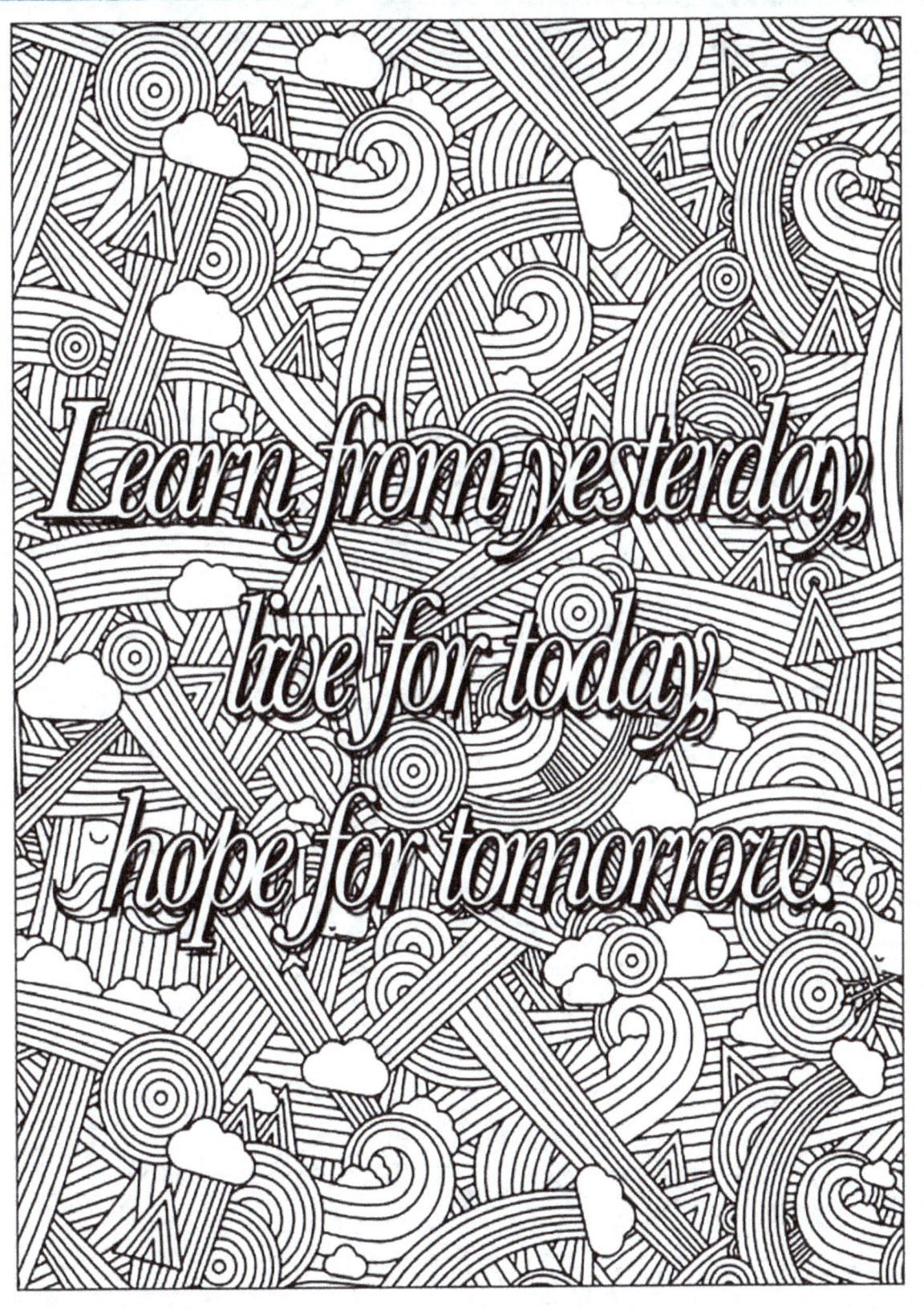

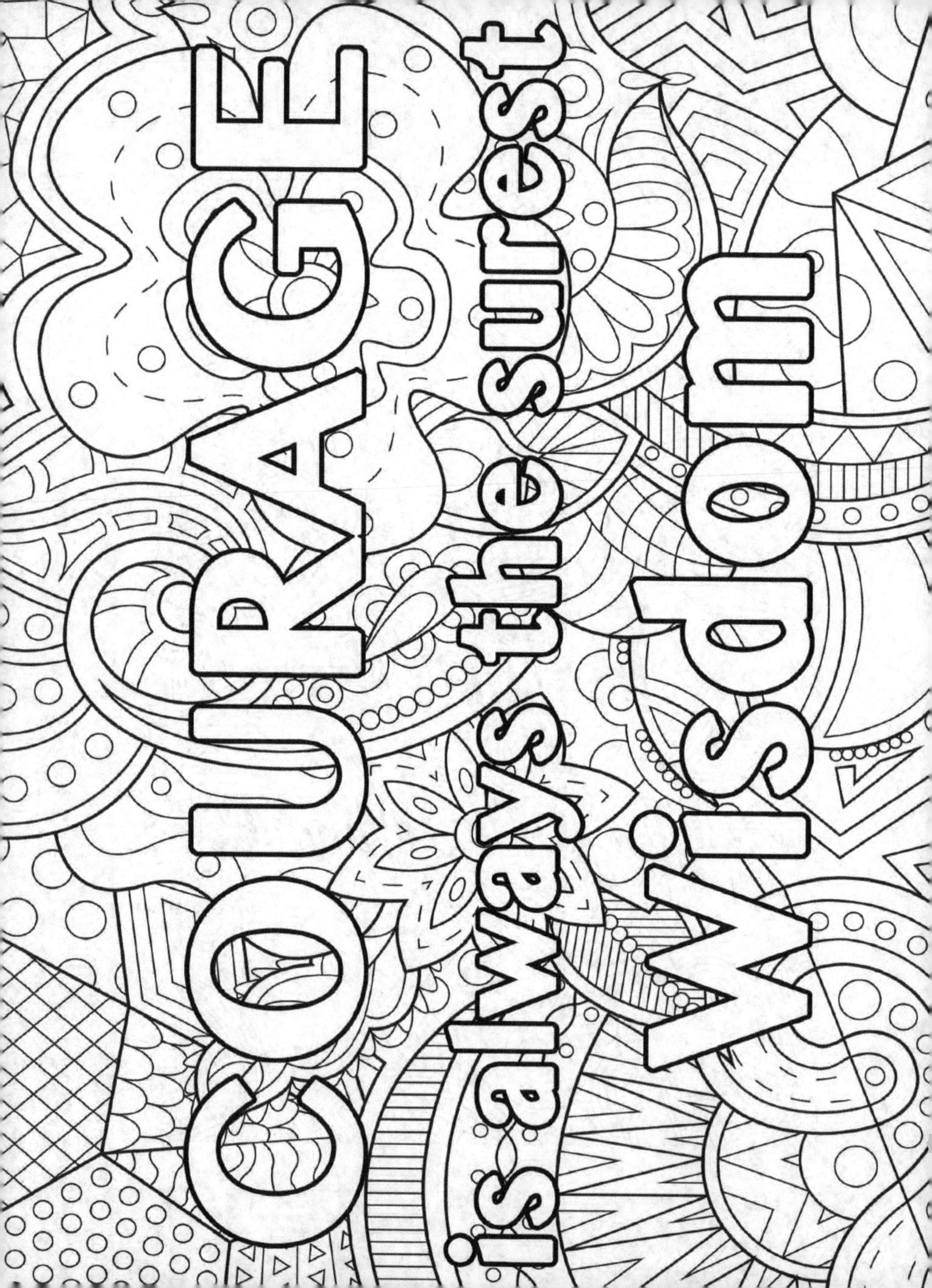

COURAGE the surest Wisdom is always surest

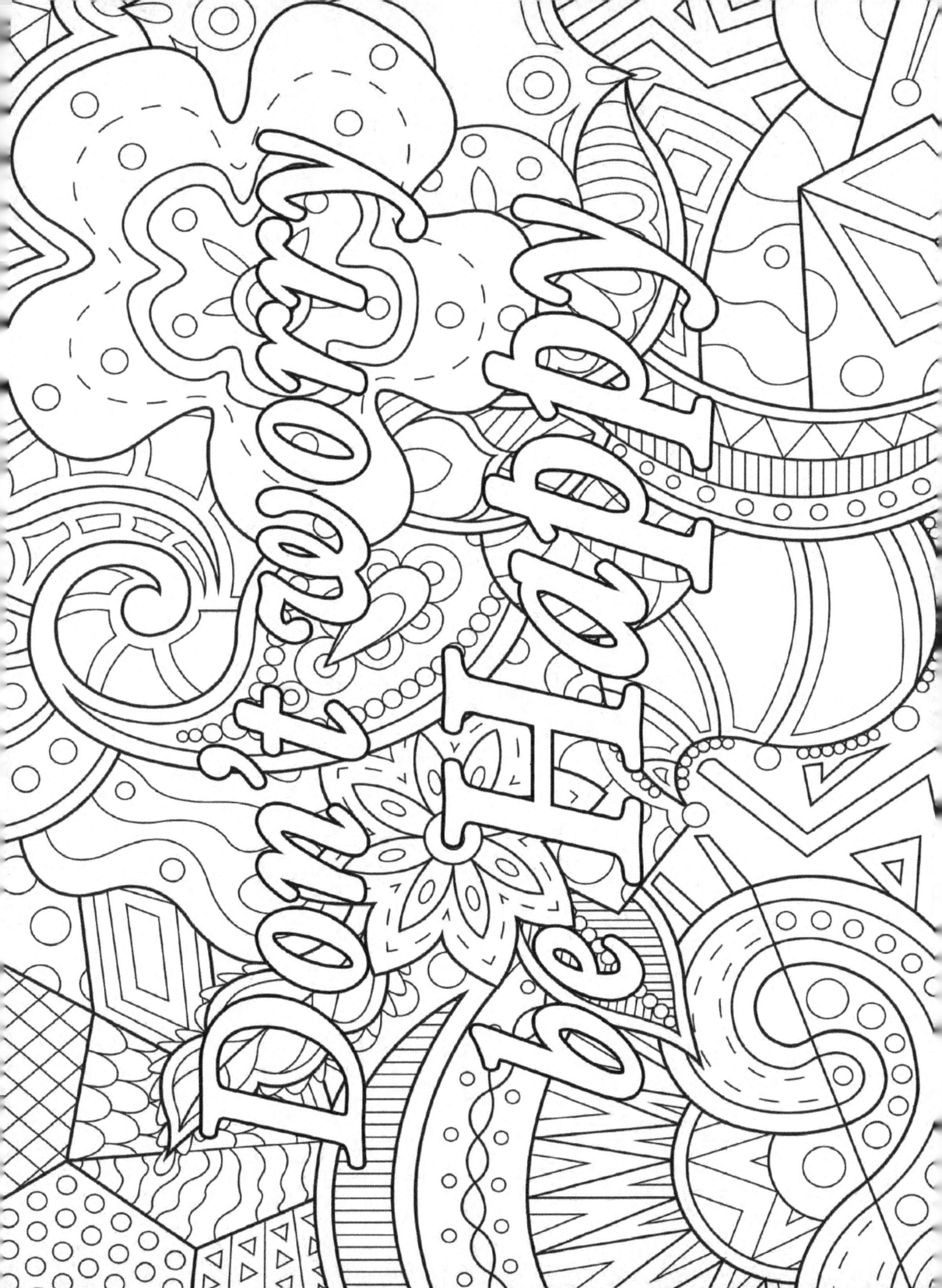

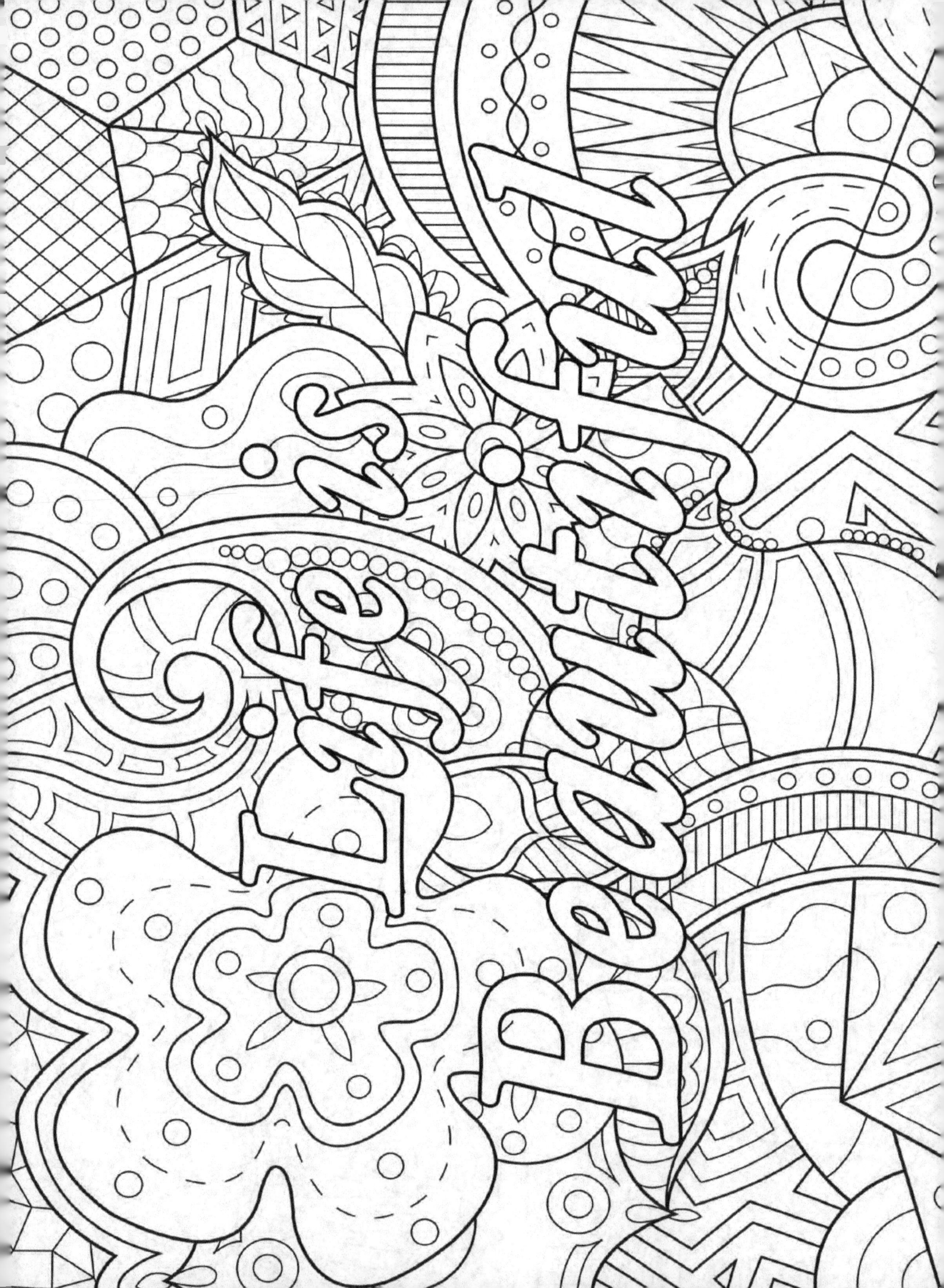

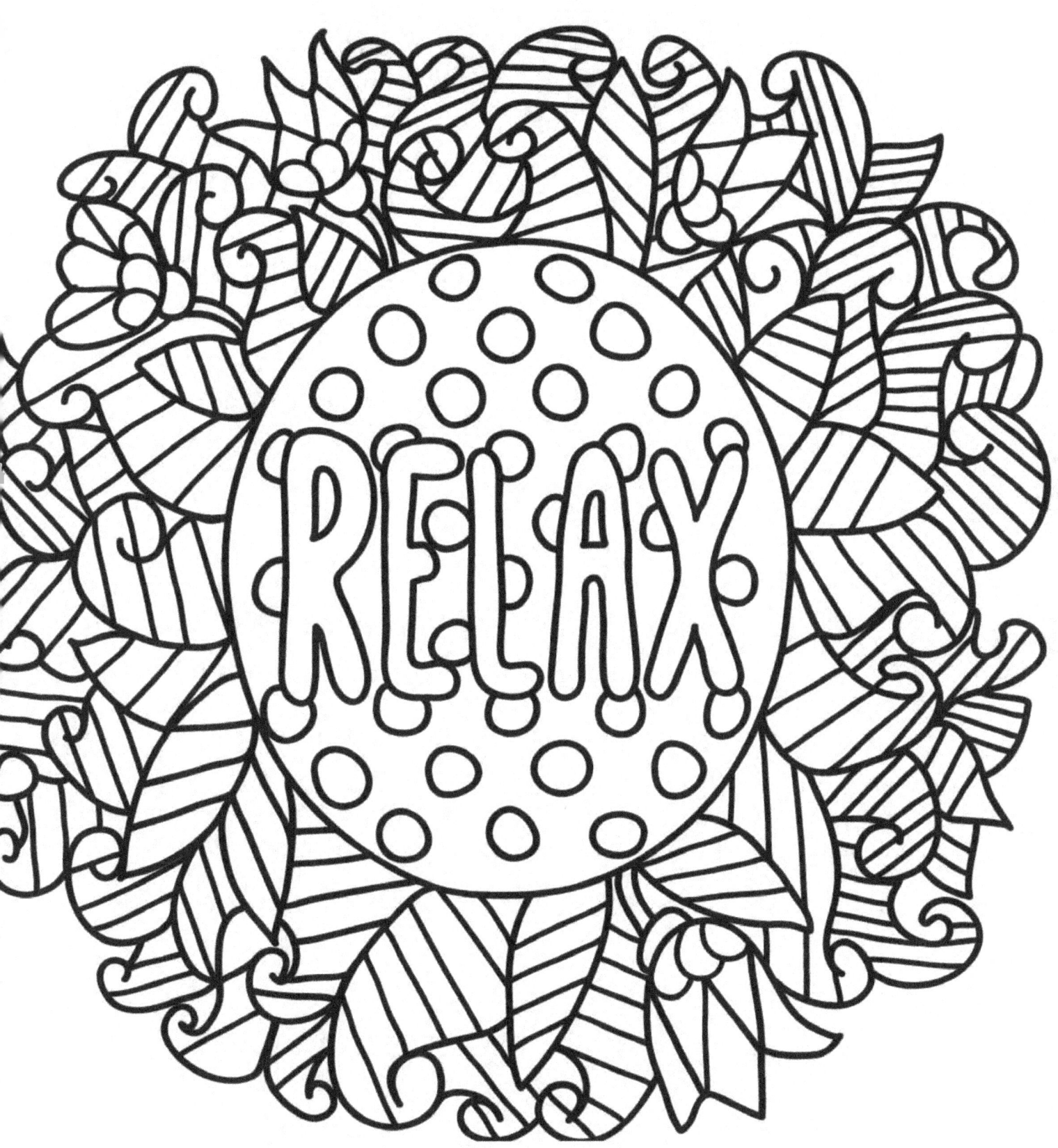

You are a SUPER hero! What is your power?
Draw a picture of your costume..

Draw your favorite shape all over the page. Color some of them and make designs in the others.

Laughter is good! Write down a few jokes. Design a big red laughing mouth on your page.

Free Write.

Randomly put 6 pieces of tape on your page. Color the page with lots of color. Take the tape off and write 6 adjectives to describe yourself in the blanks.

Take time to color

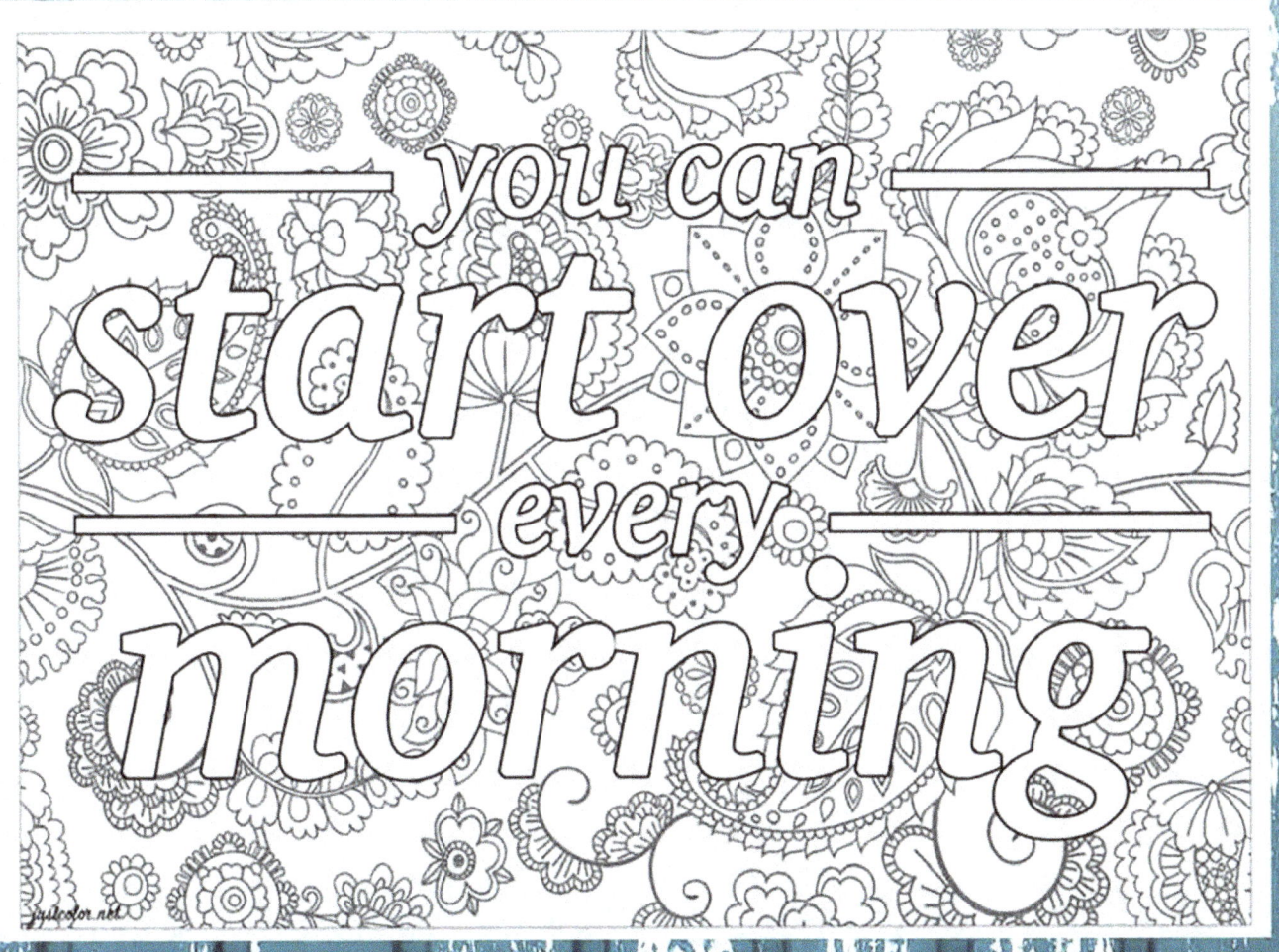

Good Morning
never forget how awesome you are

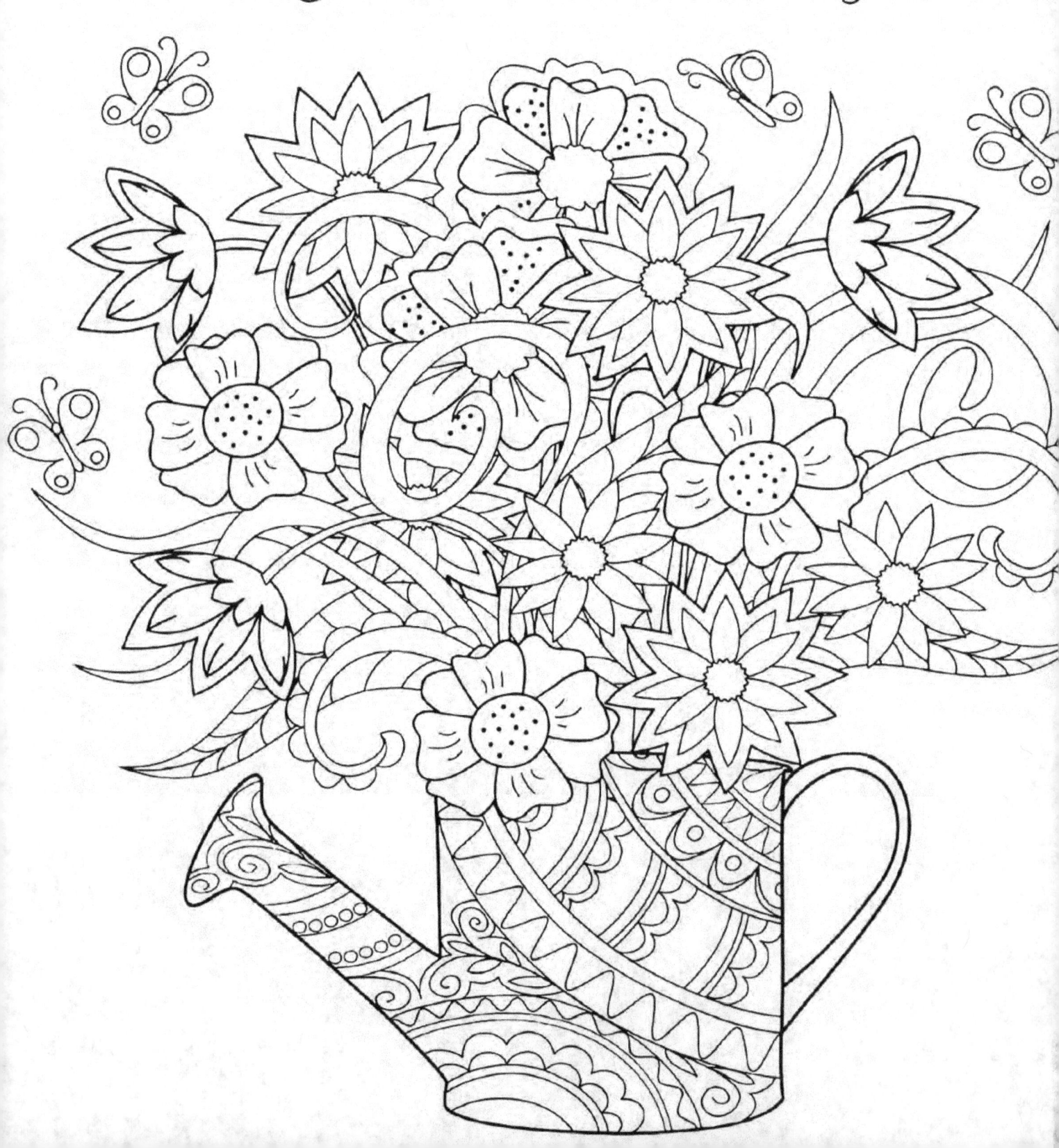

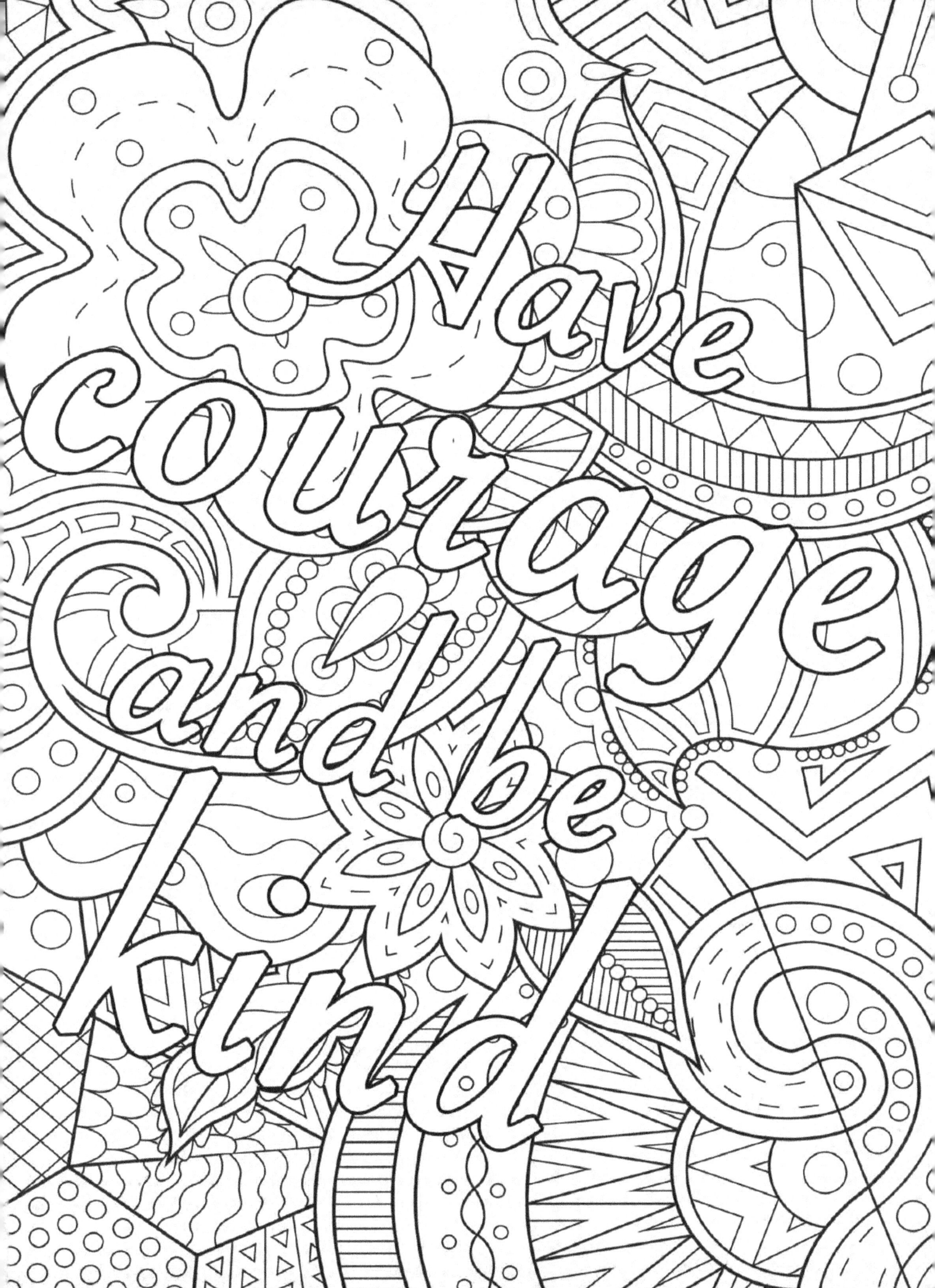

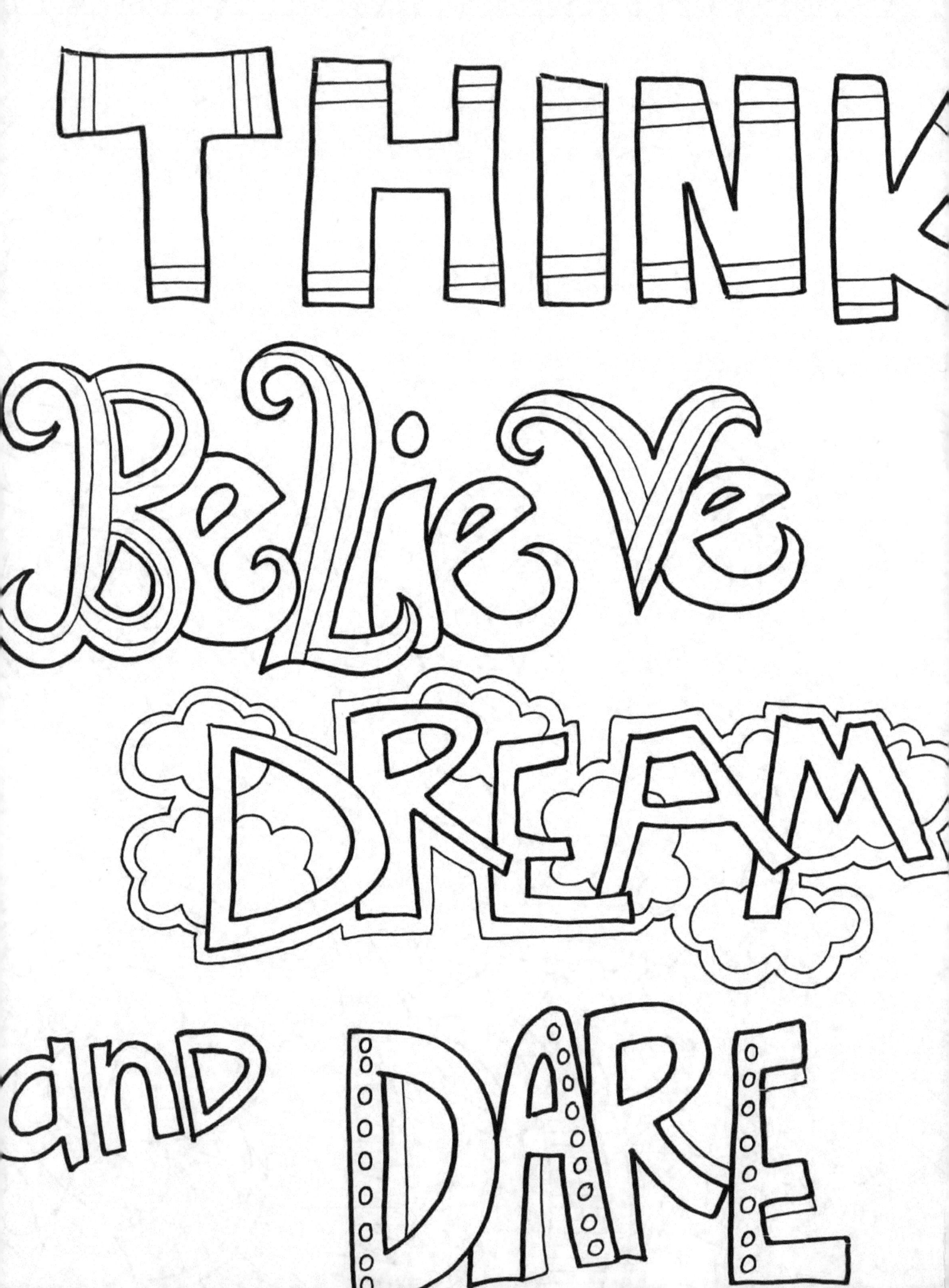

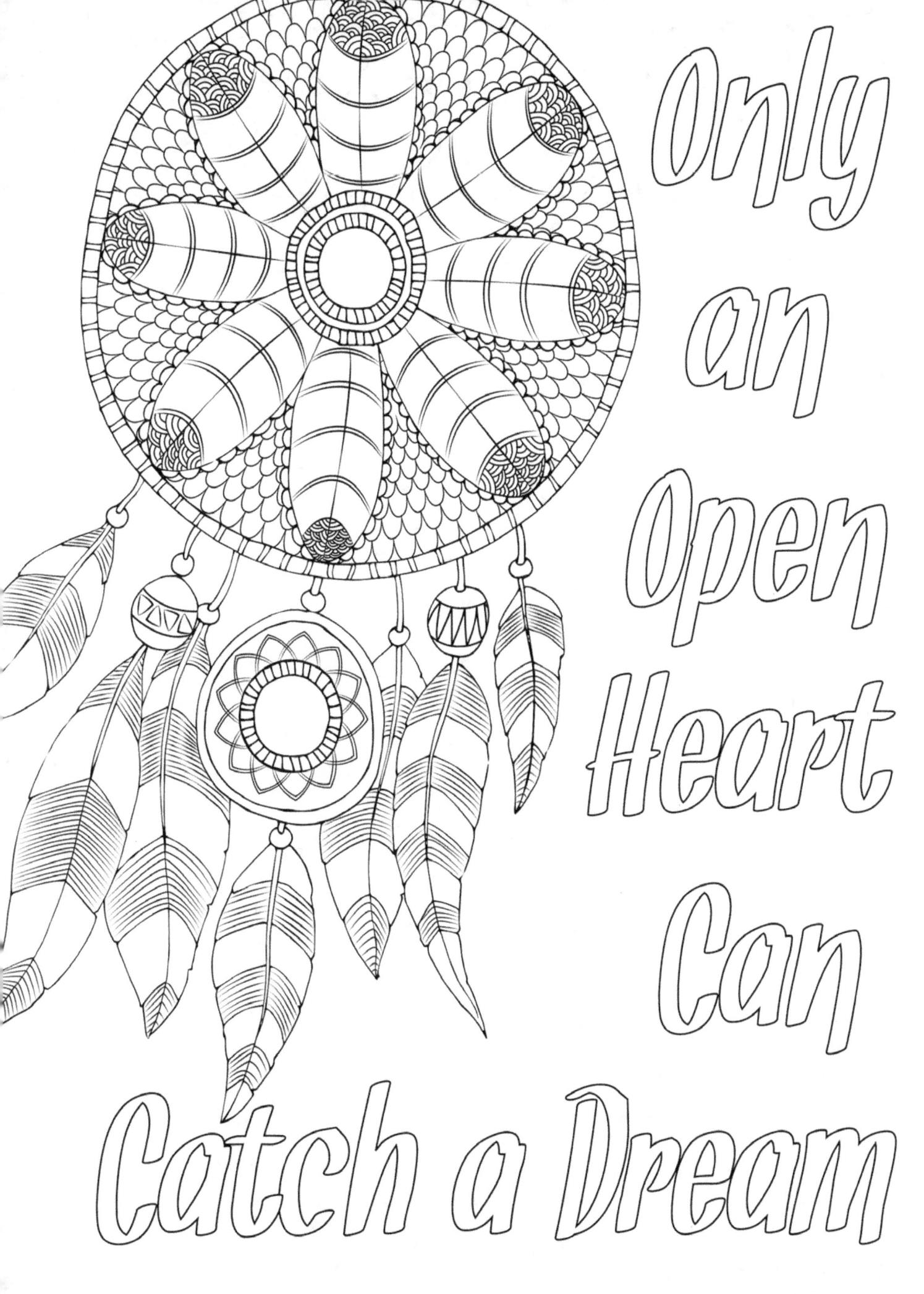

Only an Open Heart Can Catch a Dream

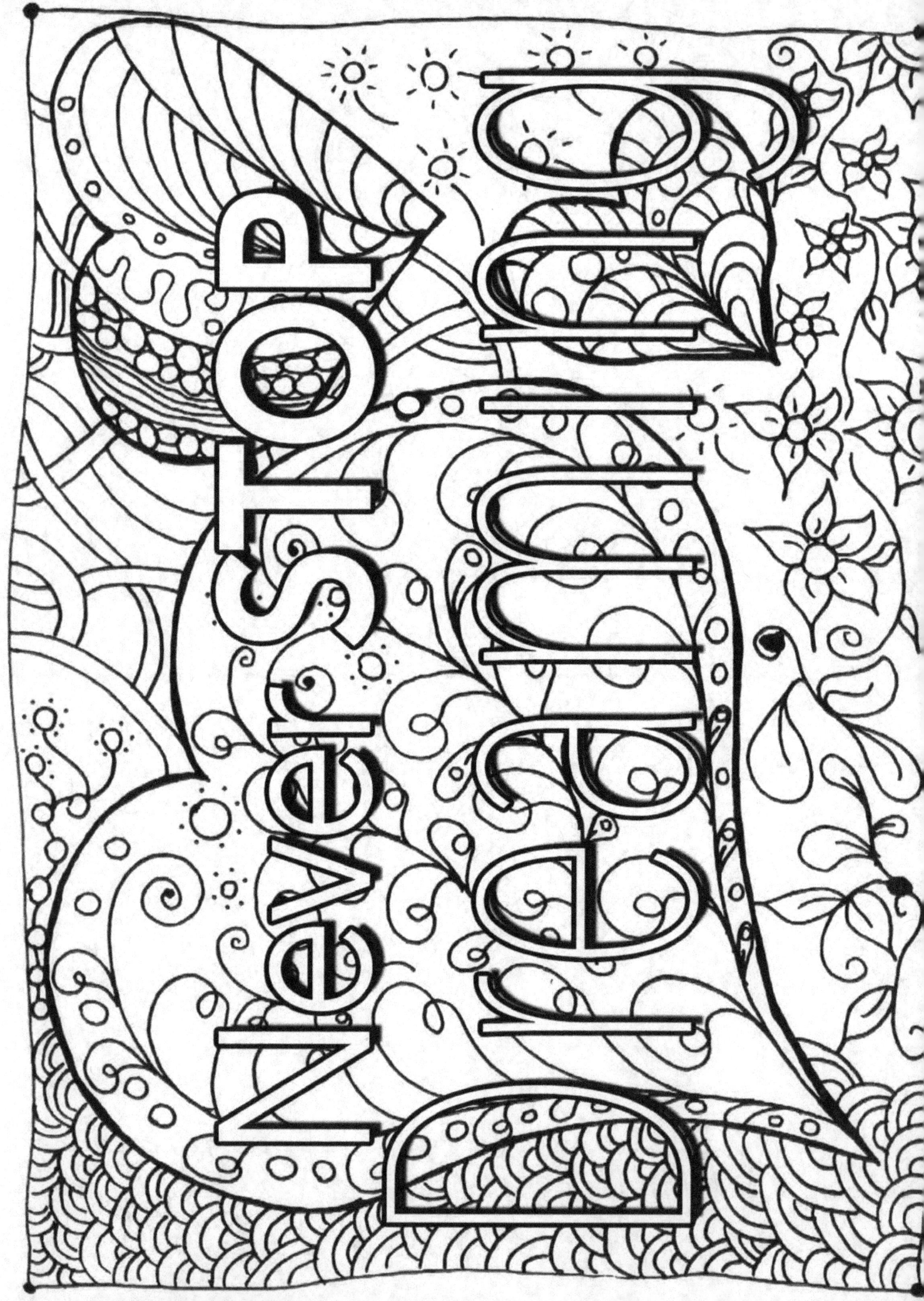

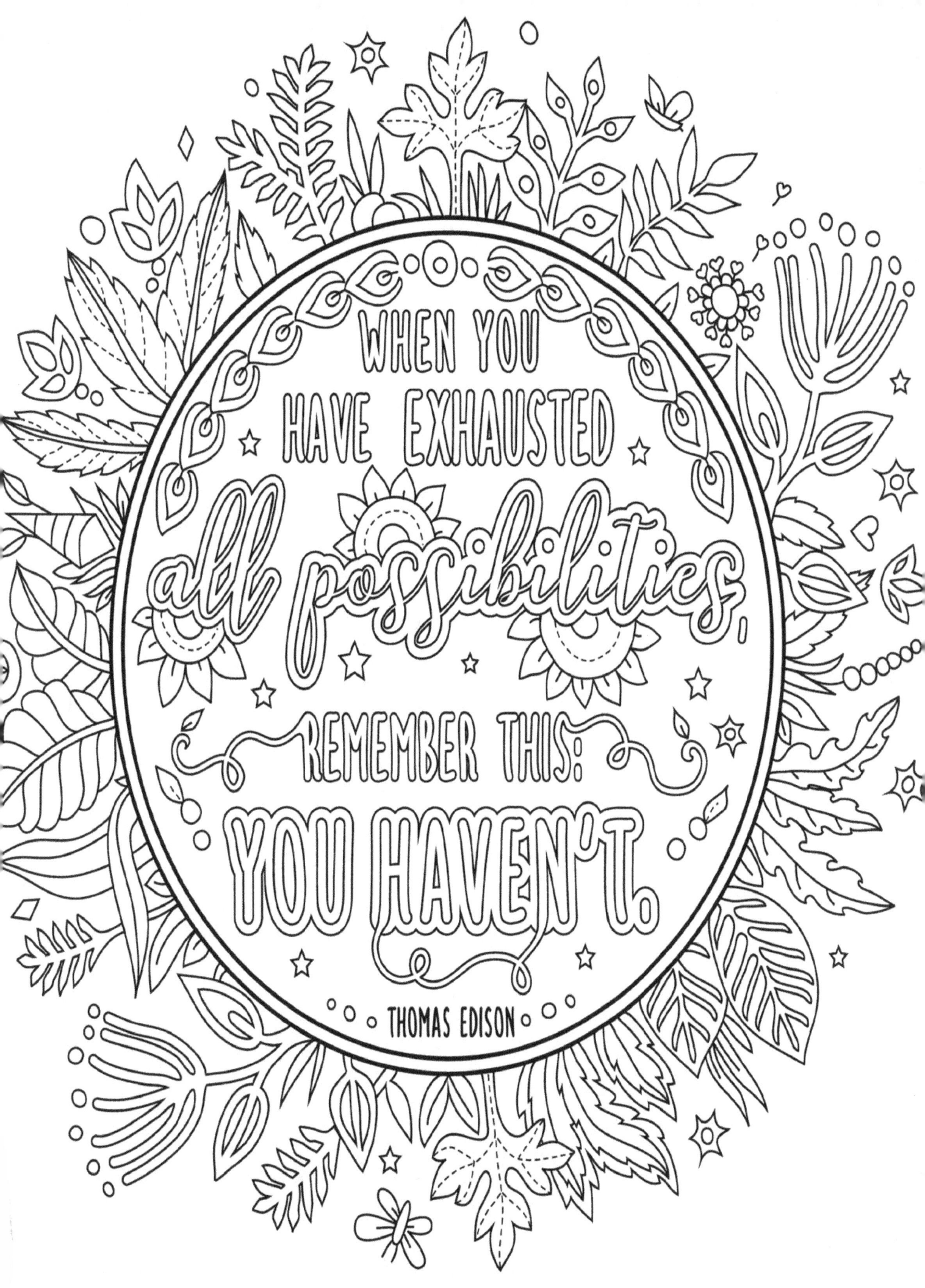